EVERY PERSON
IN THE
BOOK
OF
MORMON

EVERY PERSON
IN THE
BOOK
OF
MORMON

LYNN F. PRICE

Second Printing, April 2000

International Standard Book Number
0-88290-533-3

Horizon Publishers' Catalog and Order Number
1202

Printed and distributed
in the United States of America by

Horizon
Publishers
& Distributors, Incorporated

Mailing Address:
P.O. Box 490
Bountiful, Utah 84011-0490

Street Address:
50 South 500 West
Bountiful, Utah 84010

Phone and Fax:
Local Phone: (801) 295-9451
Toll Free: 1 (866) 818-6277
FAX: (801) 295-0196

Internet:
E-mail: horizonp@burgoyne.com
Home Page: http://www.horizonpublishersbooks.com

Table of Contents

People First Mentioned in:

Key to Understanding Markings and Codes Used in Text

There are 11 codes or markings used throughout this book: 1. *Numbers* (1 through 238); 2. *Superscript numbers*; 3. *Asterisks*; 4. *A number or word in parentheses* (1 through "Last") following a person's name in that person's initial heading: i.e., 50. * Alma² (1); 5. *CAPITALIZATION*; 6. ***Bolding***; 7. <u>*Underlining*</u>; 8. *Scriptural References*; 9. *Parentheses*; 10. *Brackets*; and 11. *References to Supplements*.

1. Numbers 1 through 238. There are 238 people or groups of people mentioned in The Book of Mormon. An entry number is assigned to each person and appears in that person's heading, indicating their order of appearance or mention in The Book of Mormon. Thus, Lehi¹, who is the very first person mentioned in The Book of Mormon [in the *Heading* to 1 Nephi], has the number **1.** preceding his name in the title of his section. His wife, Sariah, is the second person mentioned in The Book of Mormon and her name is preceded by a **2.** in the title of her section. Shiz, the last person to be mentioned by name in The Book of Mormon [in the Book of Ether] is number **238.** [Jesus Christ (#143), the Jaredites (#179), Coriantumr² (#232), Mormon² (#159) and Moroni² (#162) are mentioned long before their actual appearance in The Book of Mormon. Thus, they are briefly mentioned on pages 32, 44, 45, and 47, respectively, but the discussion of events that took place during their lives follows in the appropriate chronological order.]

Whenever people are initially referred to in someone else's narrative, their number in parentheses follows their bolded name: i.e., in Lehi's¹ narrative, when Sariah is first mentioned, her name is followed by (#2).

2. Superscript numbers are given to people who share the same name. For instance, the four people named Lehi are each designated by the superscript number that is given to him in the Index to The Book of

Mormon. The lowest number is assigned to the Lehi who was born first. Each succeeding person with that given name receives the next higher superscript number. For instance, Lehi's[1] son, Joseph, is Joseph[2] because the Joseph who was sold into Egypt by his brothers as recorded in the Old Testament is Joseph[1] since he lived in an earlier period of history than Lehi[1] and his family. Every individual who is given a superscript number has that superscript number affixed to his name whenever he is mentioned in this document so as to help the reader more easily identify and remember which Lehi or which Joseph, etc. is being referred to at the time. Therefore, Lehi[1] will always have the superscript number [1] and Lehi[2] will always bear the superscript number [2].

3. Asterisks *. An asterisk following the entry number and preceding a person's name means that person was a keeper of the records. It appears only one time for each such individual and is contained in the initial heading: i.e., **1. * LEHI**[1].

4. A number in parentheses following a name in some initial headings. This number indicates that the individual was a chief judge during the reign of the judges and identifies him by order from first to last: i.e., **50.* ALMA**[2] **(1).** The number in parentheses means that Alma[2], the 50th person mentioned in The Book of Mormon, was the first chief judge during the reign of the judges.

5. Capitalization. Each person's name is capitalized twice to emphasize that individual: first, in that person's initial heading and, second, at the very beginning of that person's narrative.

6. Bolding. Bolding is used in the following ways: (a) to highlight the person's name in the initial heading where it is both bolded and capitalized; (b) to highlight the person whose narrative it is at the beginning of that person's narrative where it is bolded, capitalized and underlined; to highlight each person referred to in any other person's narrative when that person is first mentioned in that particular narrative. Thereafter, it is not bolded.

7. Underlining. Underlining is used only at the beginning of each person's narrative to further highlight the person whose narrative it is. The person's name is capitalized, bolded, and underlined.

8. Scriptural References. The first scriptural reference denotes the exact chapter and verse where a person is first mentioned in The Book of Mormon. Scriptural references that follow usually only denote the book and chapter where the information provided can be found. These references are all *italicized* and are at the beginning of each new chapter discussed. Specific verses may be indicated within the narrative. They are set off in brackets [ ] and are not italicized.

9. Parentheses. Parentheses are used throughout the text. They are used around the numbers indicating the order in which people are initially mentioned in The Book of Mormon: i.e., in Lehi's[1] narrative, the first time another person is mentioned, that person's name is bolded and it is followed by a number in parentheses. **Sariah** is followed by (#2), **Laman**[1] is followed by (#3), etc. Parentheses are also used in some of the headings around numbers that indicate which chief judge that person was: i.e., **Alma**[2] (#50) was the first chief judge and his name is followed by (1).

10. Brackets [ ]. Brackets are used to set off explanatory information including specific scriptural references within the narrative.

11. References to Supplements. Some people mentioned in The Book of Mormon are Biblical and are not actual Book of Mormon people. They are identified in *Supplement A* (SA): i.e., Joseph[1] (SA#7), who was sold by his brothers into Egypt. Other Biblical personages are not even mentioned in The Book of Mormon but have some of the same names that Book of Mormon people have and, therefore, have superscript numbers affixed to them that precede the superscript numbers of Book of Mormon people. They are identified in *Supplement B* (SB): i.e., Jared[1] (SB#3), the father of Enoch[2]. [Enoch is not a Book of Mormon name, only Biblical. Therefore, no explanation is given regarding people with that name.] *Supplement C* (SC) contains information about Joseph Smith who is referred to in The Book of Mormon.

Foreword

The Book of Mormon is basically a family biography which retells the lives of Lehi[1] and Sariah and their posterity over a 1000-year period. It also includes the biography of another people, the Jaredites.

As with any family, from time to time certain names were passed on from generation to generation or even reappear generations later. This multiplicity of certain names can cause The Book of Mormon reader some difficulty in trying to differentiate between people who bear the same given name.

The purpose of this book is to help the reader become more familiar with people whose lives are recounted in The Book of Mormon; to be able to tell the difference between the various people bearing the same or similar names; to be able to remember the Lord's interaction with the different people; and, thereby, be able to learn and understand the lessons to be gained from each person's experiences more effectively.

Therefore, a brief synopsis of every person mentioned in The Book of Mormon, along with the appropriate scriptural references, is given in the order of their appearance or mention in The Book of Mormon. An occasional *Note* has been included that elaborates or clarifies specific information.

A special thank you is extended to Duane S. Crowther, president of Horizons Publishers, and to Lorin May, editor, for their help, encouragement and assistance in bringing the publication of this book to completion. Thanks is also extended to my husband, Dick, and my son, Russ, for their patience, long suffering and encouragement. Without their support and encouragement, I would never have been able to complete this project.

1

People First Mentioned in the Book of 1 Nephi

1.* LEHI[1]

Heading. **LEHI**[1] was a Hebrew prophet who led his followers to the promised land in the western hemisphere [c. 600 B.C.] after the **Lord** (#143) warned him to depart out of the land of Jerusalem because of the wickedness of the people. The Book of Mormon is basically the history of his people, their rise and fall, and their interactions with God. [**Lehi**[2] (#72) was the son of **Zoram**[2] (#76); **Lehi**[3] (#98) was a Nephite military commander and may be the same person as **Lehi**[2]; **Lehi**[4] (#128) was the son of **Helaman**[2] (#91).]

1 Nephi 1. Lehi[1] had many visions and dreams which he recorded. His son **Nephi**[1] (#6) abridged his record.

He departed into the wilderness about 600 B.C., leaving his house, gold, and all the precious things that they had, taking only his wife, **Sariah** (#2), his four sons [**Laman**[1] (#3), **Lemuel** (#4), **Sam** (#5) and **Nephi**[1]] and enough provisions for the journey.

1 Nephi 3. Lehi[1] sent his sons back to Jerusalem to get the brass plates from **Laban** (#7), as he was commanded to do by the Lord in a dream.

1 Nephi 5. The brass plates revealed that Lehi[1] was a descendant of **Joseph**[1] (SA #7), even that Joseph[1] who was sold into Egypt, who was the son of **Jacob**[1] (SA #8). Laban also was a descendant of Joseph[1].

1 Nephi 7. Lehi[1], commanded by the Lord, instructed his sons to return to Jerusalem and get **Ishmael**[1] (#9) and his family to join them in the wilderness so they could raise up a posterity to the Lord. Ishmael[1] and his family agreed to go with them.

1 Nephi 8. Lehi[1] saw a vision of the tree of life.

1 Nephi 10:12. Lehi[1] compared the house of Israel to an olive tree whose branches should be broken off and scattered upon all the face of the earth.

1 Nephi 16:9. After a period of time in the valley of Lemuel, Lehi[1] was instructed by the Lord to pack up and continue his journey in the wilderness. He discovered a round ball of curious workmanship, the Liahona, upon the ground in front of his tent door. Within the ball were two spindles: one pointed the direction they were to go. Messages from the Lord were written on the Liahona.

Everyone except Nephi[1] murmured against the Lord when Nephi[1] broke his bow and they could not obtain food. After Nephi[1] built a new bow, he asked his father where he should look for food. Lehi[1] inquired of the Lord, and the Lord gave instructions on the Liahona.

1 Nephi 18:7. Lehi[1] had two more sons, born in the wilderness: **Jacob**[2] (#10) and **Joseph**[2] (#11).

1 Nephi 18:17-18. Lehi[1] and his wife were brought low, almost to the point of death, while crossing the ocean on the ship their sons built because of Laman's[1] and Lemuel's constant rebellion and their binding up of Nephi[1].

1 Nephi 18:23. They landed in the promised land about 589 B.C.

2 Nephi 1:4-6. Lehi[1] saw in a vision that Jerusalem had been destroyed. He indicated that God had covenanted with him that the promised land was to be a land of inheritance for his seed forever, and also for all those who should be led out of other countries by the hand of the Lord. He prophesied that none shall come to this land except they be brought by the hand of the Lord.

2 Nephi 1:15-29. Lehi[1] indicated that he had beheld the glory of the Lord. He chastised and rebuked his sons for constantly rebelling against Nephi[1]. He then encouraged Laman[1], Lemuel, Sam, and Ishmael's[1] sons to hearken unto Nephi's[1] voice.

2 Nephi 1:30. Lehi[1] praised **Zoram**[1] (#8), Laban's servant who had fled with Nephi[1] and his brothers when they took the brass plates, for his faithful and loyal friendship to Nephi[1]. He promised Zoram[1] that his seed would be as blessed as Nephi's[1] if they stayed faithful.

2 Nephi 2:1-17. Lehi[1] spoke to Jacob[2] and indicated that Jacob[2], just in his youth, had already beheld the glory of the Lord. While talking to Jacob[2], he reminded him that redemption comes through the **Holy Messiah** (#143). He taught that freedom of choice is essential to existence and progression. He also taught that there must be opposition in all things or there could not be happiness nor misery, and there would have been no purpose for the creation.

2 Nephi 2:17-25. Lehi[1] pointed out that the devil is a fallen angel seeking that which is evil before God. He recounted the story of the fall of **Adam** (SA #4) and **Eve** (SA #5) and the necessity for the fall.

2 Nephi 2:26-30. Lehi[1] stressed that the Messiah is the great Mediator of all men.

2 Nephi 3. Lehi[1] cautioned Joseph[2] to hearken to Nephi[1]. He recounted the prophecy of Joseph[1]. Joseph[1] had prophesied that in the latter days a seer would be raised up who would carry the gospel message to Lehi's[1] posterity. This seer would be named Joseph after his father and after Joseph[1] who was captive in Egypt. In that day, that which would be written by Lehi's[1] seed [The Book of Mormon] and that which would be written by the loins of Judah [the Bible] would come together unto the confounding of false doctrines.

2 Nephi 4: 1-11. Prior to Lehi's[1] death, he counseled Laman's[1] posterity and gave them a blessing. He then called Lemuel's posterity together and counseled them and gave them a blessing, too. And then he called the sons of Ishmael[1] and their families together and spoke to them. To Sam he said, "Blessed art thou, and thy seed; for thou shalt inherit the land like unto thy brother Nephi[1]. And thy seed shall be numbered with his seed; and thou shalt be even like unto thy brother, and thy seed like unto his seed; and thou shalt be blessed in all thy days" [v. 11].

2 Nephi 4:12. Lehi[1] died and was buried.

LEHI'S[1] VISIONS AND DREAMS

He saw the Father, the Son and twelve earthly ministers, then beheld the destruction of Jerusalem [1 Nephi 1:6-14].

The Lord spoke to him in a dream and told him to take his family and leave Jerusalem [1 Nephi 2:2].

Lehi[1] dreamed a dream wherein he was commanded of the Lord to have his sons return to Jerusalem to obtain the brass plates from Laban, which plates contained the genealogy records and the record of the Jews [1 Nephi 3:2-4].

Lehi[1] saw a vision of the tree of life [1 Nephi 8:4-28].

Lehi[1] saw in a vision that Jerusalem had been destroyed [2 Nephi 1:4].

LEHI'S[1] PROPHECIES

He prophesied that the brass plates would go forth unto all nations, kindreds, tongues and people who were of his seed [1 Nephi 5:18].

Lehi[1] prophesied that after Jerusalem was destroyed and many people had been carried captive into Babylonia, they would be restored to their land of inheritance [1 Nephi 10:3].

He prophesied that 600 years from the time of his family's departure from Jerusalem, the Messiah, raised up from the Jews, would come [1 Nephi 10:4].

He told of the coming of one [John the Baptist] who would prepare the way of the Lord, and he said that this man would also baptize the Messiah [1 Nephi 10:7-9].

Lehi[1] prophesied to his family of the death and resurrection of the Savior. He told them of the things the Savior would teach and that the Savior would make himself manifest unto the Gentiles by the power of the Holy Ghost. He compared the scattering of Israel unto an olive tree [1 Nephi 10:11-14].

No one except those people who are brought by the Lord shall come unto the promised land [2 Nephi 1:6]. As long as they are righteous, they will prosper, and no one will be able to take the land from them. But, when they ripen in wickedness, the Lord will bring other nations unto them and they will take possession of the land and cause Lehi's[1] posterity to be smitten and scattered.

2. SARIAH

Heading. **SARIAH** was **Lehi's**[1] (#1) wife [c. 600 B.C.].

1 Nephi 5. When Sariah's four sons, **Laman**[1] (#3), **Lemuel** (#4), **Sam** (#5), and **Nephi**[1] (#6), were gone so long in their effort to obtain the brass plates from **Laban** (#7), Sariah feared they had perished and she murmured against her husband, calling him a visionary man.

1 Nephi 18:7. Sariah had two more sons, born in the wilderness: **Jacob**[2] (#10) and **Joseph**[2] (#11).

1 Nephi 18:17-18. Sariah and Lehi[1] were brought low, almost to the point of death, while crossing the ocean on the ship their sons built because of Laman's[1] and Lemuel's constant rebellion and their binding up of Nephi[1].

1 Nephi 18:23. They landed in the promised land about 589 B.C.

3. LAMAN¹

Heading. **LAMAN**¹ was **Lehi's**¹ (#1) eldest son. He rebelled against his parents, against his brother **Nephi**¹ (#6), and against the Lord. The Lamanite nation is named after him. He and his brother Lemuel (#4) were like unto the Jews who sought to kill their father, and they murmured against him continually. [**Laman**² (#41) was a Lamanite king and father of **Laman**³ (#42). **Laman**⁴ (#111) was a Nephite soldier.]

1 Nephi 3. Laman¹ went with his brothers back to Jerusalem to obtain the brass plates from **Laban** (#7). Laman¹ drew the lot to be the one to go in to Laban to try to get the brass plates. Laban became angry and thrust him out from his presence and threatened to kill him. Laman¹ fled. He and his brothers were about to return to their father, but Nephi¹ talked them out of it.

At Nephi's¹ suggestion, they returned to the land of their inheritance and gathered up their precious things, gold and silver, etc., and returned to Laban, who again thrust them out and sent his servants to kill them. They hid in a cavity of a rock and Laman¹ and Lemuel beat **Sam** (#5) and Nephi¹ with a rod. An angel interceded and chastised them. He told them to return to Laban and the Lord would deliver Laban into their hands. Laman¹ and Lemuel still murmured and doubted.

1 Nephi 4. [Note: When they returned this time, Nephi¹ went to get the plates and he found Laban lying drunken on the ground. The Spirit constrained him to slay Laban, indicating that it is better for one man to perish than for a nation to dwindle and perish in unbelief. Therefore, Nephi¹ smote off Laban's head with Laban's own sword. He then donned his apparel and, in the voice of Laban, had Laban's servant, **Zoram**¹ (#8), go to the treasury with him and get him the brass plates. He had Zoram¹ walk with him back to his brothers. They made Zoram¹ promise to go back into the wilderness with them.]

1 Nephi 7. Lehi¹, commanded by the Lord, instructed his sons to return to Jerusalem to bring **Ishmael**¹ (#9) and his family back into the wilderness with them so they could raise up seed unto the Lord. Laman¹, Lemuel, two of Ishmael's¹ daughters, and his two sons and their families rebelled against Nephi[1], Sam, Ishmael[1] and his wife. They bound Nephi[1] and planned to kill him. The Lord loosed Nephi's[1] bands. Laman[1] and Lemuel again sought to lay hands on him, but Ishmael's[1] wife, one of his daughters, and one of his sons, pleaded in behalf of Nephi[1], and their hearts were softened.

1 Nephi 16:7. Laman[1] took one of the daughters of Ishmael[1] to wife, as did each of his brothers. Zoram[1] also took one of Ishmael's[1] daughters to wife.

1 Nephi 16:37-39. After Ishmael's[1] death, Laman[1] talked Lemuel and Ishmael's[1] sons into joining him in a plot to kill Lehi[1] and Nephi[1] so they could return to Jerusalem. The Lord chastised them exceedingly, and they repented for a time.

1 Nephi 17:1-19. Children were born as Lehi's[1] family continued their eight-year journey in the wilderness. They arrived at a place which they called Bountiful because of its abundant fruit and wild honey. They pitched their tents by the sea shore. The Lord instructed Nephi[1] to build a ship according to the Lord's specifications and showed him where to go to find ore to make appropriate tools, etc. Again, Laman[1] and Lemuel mocked him and complained and refused to help.

1 Nephi 17:23-55. Nephi[1] strongly rebuked his brothers and reminded them of what the Lord had done for **Moses** (SA #2) and the children of Israel and how many of them had perished because of wickedness. When Laman[1] and Lemuel tried to lay their hands on Nephi[1] to throw him into the depths of the sea, he told them that whosoever laid hands upon him would wither as a dried reed, and that stopped them. The Lord then told him to stretch his hand forth to his brothers and they would not wither before him, but he would cause them to receive a shock. After receiving the shock, they repented and believed, but only for a short time.

1 Nephi 18. Laman[1] and Lemuel finally helped build the ship, and the Lord instructed them to take provisions and board the ship. Laman[1], Lemuel, the sons of Ishmael[1], and their wives became loud and rude and rebelled against Nephi[1] even to the point of binding him up. While Nephi[1] was thus bound, the compass would not work. A terrible tempest came up and the ship was driven back upon the seas. On the fourth day, the tempest was so terrible that Laman[1], Lemuel, and the others became fearful for their lives. They finally released Nephi[1] and once again repented for their actions [vs. 14-15]. They reached the promised land approximately 589 B.C.

2 Nephi 1:14-29. Lehi[1] grew old and knew he would soon die. He chastised and rebuked his sons for constantly rebelling against Nephi[1], and he encouraged them, as well as Ishmael's[1] sons, to hearken unto Nephi's[1] voice.

2 Nephi 4:1-11. Prior to Lehi's[1] death, he counseled Laman's[1] posterity and gave them a blessing. He told them that he knew that if they were brought up in the way they should go that they would not depart from that path. Therefore, if they were cursed because of the things they did due to not being taught properly, he blessed them that the curse would be removed from them and would fall upon the heads of their parents. And he blessed them that the Lord would be merciful unto them and their seed forever.

2 Nephi 5:4-25. When Nephi[1] and his followers fled to keep from being slain by Laman[1] and his supporters, those who remained with Laman[1] were called **Lamanites** (#12). The Lord caused a skin of blackness to come upon them so they would not be enticing unto Nephi's[1] people, the **Nephites** (#13). They became an idle people, full of mischief and subtlety.

4. LEMUEL

Heading. <u>LEMUEL</u> was Lehi's[1] (#1) second son. He joined with Laman[1] (#3) in rebellion against their parents, **Nephi[1]** (#6), and the Lord.

1 Nephi 3. Lemuel went with his brothers back to Jerusalem to obtain the brass plates from **Laban** (#7). When Laman[1] drew the lot to be the one to go to Laban to try to get the brass plates, Lemuel remained outside the city walls with Nephi[1] and **Sam** (#5). When Laban became angry and thrust Laman[1] out from his presence, threatening to kill him,

Laman[1] fled to join his brothers. Lemuel and Laman[1] [and possibly Sam] were about to return to their father, but Nephi[1] talked them out of it.

At Nephi's[1] suggestion, they returned to the land of their inheritance and gathered up their gold and silver and other precious things. They returned to Laban, who again thrust them out and sent his servants to kill them. They hid in a cavity of a rock. In their anger, Laman[1] and Lemuel beat Sam and Nephi[1] with a rod. An angel interceded and chastised them. He told them to return to Laban, and told them the Lord would deliver Laban into their hands. They still murmured and doubted.

1 Nephi 4. When they returned this time, Nephi[1] was the one to go to Laban. Finding Laban lying drunken on the ground, Nephi[1] followed the Spirit, which constrained him to slay Laban. Therefore, he smote off Laban's head with Laban's own sword. He then donned his apparel and, in the voice of Laban, had Laban's servant **Zoram**[1] (#8) go to the treasury with him and get the brass plates. He had Zoram[1] walk with him back to his brothers. They made Zoram[1] promise to go with them back into the wilderness.

1 Nephi 7. Lehi[1], commanded by the Lord, instructed his sons to return to Jerusalem to bring **Ishmael**[1] (#9) and his family back into the wilderness with them so they could raise up seed unto the Lord. Laman[1], Lemuel, two of Ishmael's[1] daughters, and his two sons and their families rebelled against Nephi[1], Sam, Ishmael[1] and his wife. They bound Nephi[1] and planned to kill him. The Lord loosed Nephi's[1] bands. Laman[1] and Lemuel again sought to lay hands on him, but Ishmael's[1] wife, one of his daughters, and one of his sons, pleaded in behalf of Nephi[1], and their hearts were softened.

1 Nephi 16:7. Lemuel took one of the daughters of Ishmael[1] to wife, as did each of his brothers. Zoram[1] also took one of Ishmael's[1] daughters to wife.

1 Nephi 16:37-39. After Ishmael's[1] death, Laman[1] talked Lemuel and Ishmael's[1] sons into joining him in a plot to kill Lehi[1] and Nephi[1] so they could all return to Jerusalem. The Lord chastised them exceedingly, and they repented for a time.

1 Nephi 17:1-19. Children were born as Lemuel and his family continued their eight-year journey in the wilderness. They arrived at a place they named Bountiful because of its abundant fruit and wild honey. They pitched their tents by the sea shore. The Lord instructed Nephi[1] to build a ship according to the Lord's specifications and showed him where to go to find ore to make appropriate tools, etc. Again, Lemuel and Laman[1] mocked Nephi[1] and complained and refused to help.

1 Nephi 17:23-55. Nephi[1] strongly rebuked both Lemuel and Laman[1] and reminded them of what the Lord had done for **Moses** (SA #2) and the children of Israel, and how many of them had perished because of wickedness. When Lemuel and Laman[1] tried to lay their hands on Nephi[1] to throw him into the depths of the sea, he told them that whosoever laid hands upon him would wither as a dried reed. That stopped them. The Lord then told Nephi[1] to stretch his hand forth to his brothers and they would not wither before him. However, they would receive a shock. After getting shocked, Lemuel and Laman[1] repented and believed again for a short time.

1 Nephi 18. Lemuel and Laman[1] finally helped build the ship. The Lord instructed them to take provisions and board the ship. Lemuel, Laman[1], the sons of Ishmael[1], and their wives became loud and rude and rebelled against Nephi[1]. They bound him up. While Nephi[1] was thus bound, the compass would not work, and the ship was driven back upon the seas by a terrible tempest. The brothers began to fear for their lives. The storm became exceedingly sore [v. 14] on the fourth day and they began to see that the judgments of God were upon them. They decided they had better repent or they would perish; therefore, they released Nephi[1] and once again repented for their actions. They reached the promised land approximately 589 B.C.

2 Nephi 1:14-29. Lehi[1] grew old and knew he would soon die. He rebuked his sons for constantly rebelling against Nephi[1]. He encouraged Lemuel, Laman[1], Sam and Ishmael's[1] sons to hearken unto Nephi's[1] voice.

2 Nephi 4:1-11. Prior to Lehi's[1] death, he called Lemuel's and Laman's[1] posterity together and counseled them and gave them blessings. He told them that he knew that if they were brought up in the way they should go that they would not depart from that path. Therefore, he blessed them that, if they were cursed due to not being taught properly, the curse would be removed from them and would fall upon the heads of their parents.

5. SAM

Heading. <u>SAM</u> was **Lehi's**[1] (#1) third son.

1 Nephi 3. Sam went with his brothers back to Jerusalem to obtain the brass plates from **Laban** (#7). When **Laman**[1] (#3) drew the lot to be the one to go in to Laban to try to get the brass plates, Sam remained with **Lemuel** (#4) and **Nephi**[1] (#6) outside the city wall. When Laban became angry and thrust Laman[1] out from his presence, threatening to kill him, Laman[1] fled to join his brothers. Laman[1] and Lemuel [and possibly Sam] were about to return to their father, but Nephi[1] talked them out of it.

At Nephi's[1] suggestion, they returned to the land of their inheritance and gathered up their gold, silver, and other precious things. They returned to Laban, who again thrust them out and sent his servants to kill them. They hid in a cavity of a rock. Laman[1] and Lemuel beat Sam and Nephi[1] with a rod. An angel interceded and chastised them. He told them to return to Laban, and the Lord would deliver Laban into their hands. Laman[1] and Lemuel still murmured and doubted.

1 Nephi 4. When they returned this time, Nephi[1] went to Laban. He found him lying drunken on the ground. The Spirit constrained him to slay Laban, indicating that it is better for one man to perish than for a nation to dwindle and perish in unbelief. Therefore, Nephi[1] smote off Laban's head with Laban's own sword. He then donned his apparel and, in the voice of Laban, had Laban's servant **Zoram**[1] (#8) go to the treasury with him and get him the brass plates. He had Zoram[1] walk with him back to his brothers. They made Zoram[1] promise to go with them back into the wilderness.

1 Nephi 7. Lehi[1], commanded by the Lord, then instructed his sons to return to Jerusalem to bring **Ishmael**[1] (#9) and his family back with them so they could raise seed up unto the Lord. Laman[1], Lemuel, two of Ishmael's[1] daughters, and his two sons and their families rebelled against

Nephi[1], Sam, and Ishmael[1] and his wife. They bound Nephi[1] and planned to kill him. The Lord loosed Nephi's[1] bands. Laman[1] and Lemuel again sought to lay hands on him, but Ishmael's[1] wife, one of his daughters, and one of his sons pleaded in behalf of Nephi[1], and their hearts were softened.

1 Nephi 16:7. Lehi's[1] sons and Zoram[1] took Ishmael's[1] daughters to wife, with Zoram[1] taking the eldest daughter to wife.

2 Nephi 1:14-29. Lehi[1] grew old and knew he would soon die. He rebuked his sons for constantly rebelling against Nephi[1]. He encouraged Laman[1], Lemuel, Sam and Ishmael's[1] sons to hearken unto Nephi's[1] voice.

2 Nephi 4:1-11. Prior to Lehi's[1] death, he called Laman[1] and Lemuel, and Ishmael's[1] sons, and all of their posterity together and counseled them and gave them blessings. To Sam he said, "Blessed art thou, and thy seed; for thou shalt inherit the land like unto thy brother Nephi[1]. And thy seed shall be numbered with his seed; and thou shalt be even like unto thy brother, and thy seed like unto his seed; and thou shalt be blessed in all thy days" [v. 11].

Alma 3:6. We are reminded in Alma 3:6 that Nephi[1], Jacob[2], Joseph[2] and Sam were just and holy men.

Note: Very little is really said about Sam. Throughout the years he and his family are alive, we do not hear him complain, nor do we ever read any direct quotation of his. Even though he is older than Nephi[1], when he and his brothers are referred to, he is sometimes listed last, as in Alma 3:6: "And the skins of the Lamanites were dark, according to the mark which was set upon their fathers, which was a curse upon them because of their rebellion against their brethren, who consisted of Nephi, Jacob, and Joseph, and Sam, who were just and holy men."

We hear of groups of people, such as Lamanites, Lemuelites, Nephites, Jacobites and Josephites, but there are no Sammites. We read that Nephi[1] consecrated Jacob[2] and Joseph[2] to be priests and teachers over the people, but we do not see any indication that Sam was ever called to the ministry.

6.* NEPHI[1]

Heading. **NEPHI**[1] was **Lehi's**[1] (#1) fourth son. He was righteous and obedient to the Lord. [The Nephite nation was comprised of those people who followed Nephi[1] and the teachings of **Jesus** (#143). **Nephi**[2] (#127) was the son of **Helaman**[3] (#118); **Nephi**[3] (#137) was the son of Nephi[2]; **Nephi**[4] (#155) was the son of Nephi[3].]

1 Nephi 1. Nephi[1] was taught in all the learning of his father. He made a record in the language of his father, which was a mixture of the learning of the Jews and the language of the Egyptians [v. 2]. He abridged the record of his father and then made a record of those things that happened during his lifetime.

1 Nephi 2. Nephi[1] was exceedingly young at the time his family left Jerusalem. Nevertheless, he was large in stature and very close to the Lord. He indicated that the Lord "did visit me and . . . soften my heart that I did believe all the words which had been spoken by my father, wherefore, I did not rebel against him like my brothers" [v. 16].

The Lord told Nephi[1] that they would be led to a land of promise and that, if his brothers rebelled against him, they would be cut off. He was also told that, inasmuch as he kept the commandments, he would be made a ruler and teacher over his brothers.

1 Nephi 3. When Lehi[1] told Nephi[1] that the Lord had told him in a dream that Nephi[1] and his brethren needed to return to Jerusalem to obtain the brass plates from **Laban** (#7), Nephi[1] said he would go because he knew the Lord would give no commandments unto the children of men save he would prepare a way for them to accomplish the thing which he, the Lord, had commanded them.

They had difficulty obtaining the plates from Laban. When Laman[1] (#3) fled from Laban's house and he and his brothers wanted to return empty-handed to their father, Nephi[1] talked them out of it and suggested they get some of their riches and buy the record from Laban. When they returned to Laban, he thrust them out and sent his servants to slay them. They fled, leaving their possessions behind. They hid in the cavity of a rock. Laman[1] and **Lemuel** (#4) beat Nephi[1] and **Sam** (#5) with a rod. An angel interceded and told them to return to Jerusalem and the Lord would deliver Laban into their hands.

1 Nephi 4. When they returned this time, Nephi[1] found Laban lying drunken on the ground. The Spirit constrained him to slay Laban, indicating that it is better for one man to perish than for a nation to dwindle and perish in unbelief. Therefore, Nephi[1] cut Laban's head off with Laban's own sword. He then donned his apparel and, in the voice of Laban, had Laban's servant **Zoram**[1] (#8) go to the treasury with him and get him the brass plates. He had Zoram[1] walk with him back to his brothers. They then made Zoram[1] promise to go with them back into the wilderness.

1 Nephi 7. Lehi[1], commanded by the Lord, then instructed his sons to return to Jerusalem to bring Ishmael[1] (#9) and his family back with them so they could raise seed up unto the Lord. Laman[1], Lemuel, two of Ishmael's[1] daughters, and his two sons and their families rebelled against Nephi[1], Sam, and Ishmael[1] and his wife. They bound Nephi[1] and planned to kill him. The Lord loosed Nephi's[1] bands. Laman[1] and Lemuel again sought to lay hands on him, but Ishmael's[1] wife, one of his daughters, and one of his sons, pleaded in behalf of Nephi[1], and their hearts were softened.

1 Nephi 9. Nephi[1] made two sets of plates: one contained the secular history, the other contained the religious history.

1 Nephi 15:12-20. Nephi[1] explained to his brothers what his father meant when he compared the house of Israel to an olive tree. He also quoted **Isaiah**[1] (SA #11) to them.

1 Nephi 15:21-36. Nephi[1] interpreted Lehi's[1] vision of the tree of life for his brothers.

1 Nephi 16:7. Nephi[1] and his brothers each took one of the daughters of Ishmael[1] to wife, as did Zoram[1].

1 Nephi 16:18. Nephi's[1] bow broke while he was hunting for food. His brothers became angry with him. Everyone, except Nephi[1], murmured against the Lord because of their hardships and lack of food. Nephi[1] made a new bow out of wood and inquired of his father where he should go to look for food. His father inquired of the Lord, and the Liahona gave directions to them.

1 Nephi 16:37-39. After Ishmael[1] died, Laman[1] encouraged Lemuel and the sons of Ishmael[1] to join him in a plot to kill Lehi[1] and Nephi[1] so they could return to Jerusalem. The Lord chastised them exceedingly, and they repented.

1 Nephi 17:1-19. Children were born as Lehi's[1] family continued their eight-year journey in the wilderness. They arrived at a place called Bountiful because of its abundant fruit and wild honey. They pitched their tents by the sea shore. The Lord instructed Nephi[1] to build a ship according to the Lord's specifications and showed him where to go to find ore to make appropriate tools, etc. Again, Nephi's[1] brothers mocked him and complained and refused to help.

1 Nephi 17:23-55. Nephi[1] strongly rebuked his brothers and reminded them of what the Lord had done for Moses (SA #2) and the children of Israel and how many of them had perished because of wickedness. When his brothers tried to lay their hands on him to throw him into the depths of the sea, they stopped when he told them that whosoever laid hands upon him would wither as a dried reed. The Lord then told him to stretch his hand forth to his brothers and they would not wither before him. However, the Lord indicated that he would cause them to receive a shock. Again, Laman[1] and Lemuel repented and believed, for a short time.

1 Nephi 18. Nephi[1], with the help of his brethren and with guidance from the Lord, built the ship. The Lord instructed them to take provisions and board the ship. Laman[1], Lemuel, Ishmael's[1] sons, and their wives became loud and rude on the ship and rebelled against Nephi[1]. When they bound Nephi[1] with cords, the compass ceased to work and the ship was driven back upon the seas by a terrible tempest. Laman[1], Lemuel and the others became fearful for their lives. The tempest became exceedingly sore on the fourth day [v. 14] and they began to realize that they would perish if they did not repent; thus, they released Nephi[1]. They reached the promised land approximately 589 B.C.

1 Nephi 19. The Lord commanded Nephi[1] to make plates of ore and to record on them the ministry and the prophecies. These records were to be passed down from prophet to prophet. Nephi[1] read many things to his people from that which was engraven on the plates of brass so that they would know of the Lord's dealings with people in other lands. He read to them from the books of Moses.

1 Nephi 20-21. In order to persuade his people even more to believe in the Lord, Nephi[1] read some of Isaiah's[1] (SA #11) words to them. They refer to Israel being a chosen people, that the Messiah shall be a light to the Gentiles, that Israel will be gathered in the last days, and that kings and queens shall be their nursing fathers and mothers [Isaiah 20-21].

1 Nephi 22. Nephi[1] explained the meaning of the words of Isaiah[1] that he had read to his brethren. He explained about the scattering and subsequent gathering of Israel. He also taught them that the wicked shall burn as stubble, the kingdom of the devil shall be destroyed, and Satan shall be bound.

2 Nephi 4:13-35. After Lehi's[1] death, Laman[1], Lemuel and the two sons of Ishmael[1] were angry with Nephi[1] again because of his admonitions. In Psalm-like fashion, Nephi[1] expressed his anguish caused by his own weaknesses and iniquities; then he praised the Lord and said that he put his trust in him forever.

2 Nephi 5:5-14. The Lord warned Nephi[1] that he and all those who would go with him should flee because Laman[1] and Lemuel sought to take his life. He took Sam, Jacob[2] (#10), Joseph[2] (#11), his sisters, Zoram[1], and their families, and all others who were faithful. They called themselves the people of Nephi (or Nephites, #13). Those who stayed behind were called the Lamanites (#12). In addition to their tents, etc., they took the records, the ball (or compass), and the sword of Laban with them.

2 Nephi 5:15-17. They built buildings and worked in all manner of wood, iron, copper, brass, steel, gold, silver and precious ores. They built a temple after the manner of Solomon's temple of the Old Testament.

2 Nephi 5:18. The people desired Nephi[1] to be their king, but he would not. He served them without being king.

2 Nephi 5:26. Nephi[1] consecrated Jacob[2] and Joseph[2] to be priests and teachers over the people.

2 Nephi 5:28-34. Thirty years had passed since Lehi[1] and his family left Jerusalem. It was now approximately 569 B.C. The Lord told Nephi[1] to make additional plates. By the time 40 years had passed away [559 B.C.], there had already been wars and contentions with the Lamanites.

2 Nephi 31:5-13. Nephi[1] discussed the purpose of baptism and why the Savior, himself, being perfect, was baptized: to fulfill all righteousness; to demonstrate to the children of men that, according to the flesh, he humbleth himself before the Father, and witnesseth unto the Father that he would be obedient unto him in keeping his commandments.

2 Nephi 31:19-21. Nephi[1] said he heard a voice from the Father saying that he that endureth to the end shall be saved. Repentance and baptism are the gate to the strait and narrow path which leads to eternal life.

2 Nephi 32. Nephi[1] continued to teach the people. Men must pray for themselves and gain knowledge through the Holy Ghost. People must not perform anything unto the Lord save in the first place they pray unto the Father in the name of Christ, that he will consecrate their performance unto them, that their performance may be for the welfare of their souls.

2 Nephi 33. When people speak by the power of the Holy Ghost, the power of the Holy Ghost carries it unto the hearts of the children of men if they have not hardened their hearts against the Holy Spirit. Nephi's[1] words are true. Those who believe in Christ will believe Nephi's[1] words. They will stand as a witness at the judgment bar.

Jacob 1. Nephi[1] grew old. Approximately 55 years after they left Jerusalem, he passed the records on to his brother Jacob[2]. Prior to his death, he anointed a man to be a king and a ruler over his people according to the reigns of the kings. They were called second Nephi, third Nephi, etc., in remembrance of the name of Nephi[1]. Nephi[1] died [v. 12].

Alma 3:6. Later prophets indicated that Nephi[1], Jacob[2], Joseph[2] and Sam were just and holy men.

NEPHI'S[1] VISIONS AND DREAMS

Nephi[1] saw the vision of the tree of life, as did his father, Lehi[1]. He also saw the Spirit of the Lord, the Son of God. In the vision, he saw a beautiful virgin, the mother of the Son of God, and he saw the virgin bearing a child in her arms, the Lamb of God. He was given an understanding of the vision of the tree of life. He beheld the Savior and his baptism, his ministry, the people's rejection, the twelve apostles, and the crucifixion [1 Nephi 11].

Nephi[1] beheld the land of promise and the seed of his brethren: their wickedness, their wars and destruction. He saw the events that would take place at the time of the Savior's crucifixion. He saw the Savior's appearance to those who survived the destruction and the subsequent selection of the twelve disciples of the Lamb, and received further understanding of the vision of the tree of life. He also saw the seed of his brethren dwindle in unbelief and become a dark and loathsome and filthy people, full of idleness and all manner of abominations [1 Nephi 12].

He saw the nations and kingdoms of the Gentiles and the formation of a great church whose founder was the devil. He saw the discovery and colonizing of America and the scattering of the seed of his brethren. He saw the people coming from many lands across the waters to the promised land, and he beheld the War of Independence and the victory by the colonists. He beheld a book [the Bible] that it went forth, but that many of the plain and most precious parts had been taken away from it. He saw the Gentile apostasy, the restoration of the gospel and the coming forth of latter-day scripture [The Book of Mormon]. These latter-day scriptures and the Bible would support and strengthen each other [1 Nephi 13].

He beheld the great and abominable church. There are only two churches: the church of the devil and the church of the Lamb of God. The great and abominable church sat upon many waters and had dominion over all the earth, among all nations, kindreds, tongues, and people. The church of the Lamb of God had few members. Nevertheless, it also was upon all the face of the earth. The saints of God in all the nations suffered persecution by those of the devil's church. Nephi[1] saw that there were wars and rumors of wars among all the nations which belonged to the mother of abominations. When these events occur, it will be an indication that the Father will commence in preparing the way for the fulfilling of his covenants to the house of Israel. Nephi[1] saw that the apostle John would write concerning the end of the world and his writing would be contained in the Bible [1 Nephi 14].

NEPHI'S[1] PROPHECIES

Nephi[1] prophesied that the Lord would come in 600 years from the time they left Jerusalem. He would be judged as a thing of naught. He would be scourged and smitten and spat upon. He would be crucified and buried in a sepulchre. There would be three days of darkness, which would be a sign given of his death unto those who should inhabit the isles of the sea, and especially to those who are of the house of Israel. He would then visit the house of Israel: there would be thunderings and lightnings, tempest and fire, the opening of the earth, and mountains would be carried up. The rocks of the earth would rend. The people in Jerusalem would be scourged by all people because they crucified the God of Israel; they would wander and become a hiss and a byword and be hated among all nations. Nevertheless, he prophesied that the day would come when the Holy One of Israel would remember the covenants which he made to their fathers and they would be gathered in from the four quarters of the earth and be restored to the land of their inheritance [1 Nephi 19].

Nephi[1] prophesied that all the Jews who remained in Jerusalem when Lehi[1] and his family left had been destroyed except those who were carried away captive into Babylon. Nevertheless, they would eventually be restored to the land of their inheritance. There would be wars and rumors of wars at the time the Savior manifested himself in the flesh. The Jews would reject the Savior and crucify him. He would be laid in a sepulchre and rise from the dead in three days. All who believe on his name will be saved in the kingdom of God. He further prophesied that after the Messiah manifested himself unto his people, Jerusalem would again be destroyed and the Jews would be scattered throughout all the world. After many generations, when the Jews come to accept Christ, they will be restored again to their land. The Messiah would first come 600 years from the time Lehi[1] and his family left Jerusalem. His name would be **Jesus Christ** (#143), the Son of God [2 Nephi 25].

Nephi[1] continued his prophecy: After Christ rises from the dead, he will show himself unto the Nephites. Signs will be given to the Nephites pertaining to both Christ's birth and to his death and resurrection. There will be much destruction at the time of his death, and the wicked will be destroyed. By four generations after the coming of Christ, the Nephites will have become so wicked that a speedy destruction will come to them [2 Nephi 26].

The voice of the prophets shall speak from the dust in the latter days.

In the latter days, darkness will cover the earth and there will be many false churches and much wickedness. A book [The Book of Mormon] will come forth, and it will contain the words written by those who have slumbered. The book will be sealed. It will contain a revelation from God, from the beginning of the world to the ending thereof. The sealed portion of the book will not be delivered in the day of wickedness, but shall be kept from the people.

This book [the gold plates] will be delivered unto a man [Joseph Smith] chosen of the Lord. He will dictate the words to another person. But the words that are sealed he will not dictate, nor will he give the book [the gold plates] to the other person. The day will come when the words of the book that was sealed shall be read upon the house tops, by the power of Christ, and all things shall be revealed unto the children of men. Three witnesses, chosen by the Lord, will also behold the book [the gold plates]. They will testify of its truthfulness. [Oliver Cowdery, David Whitmer, and Martin Harris, in the Introduction to The Book of Mormon, testify: "Be it known unto all nations, kindreds, tongues, and people, unto whom this work shall come: That we, through the grace of God the Father, and our Lord Jesus Christ, have seen the plates which contain this record . . ."] No one else will be allowed to view the book [the gold plates] except a "few according to the will of God, to bear testimony of his word unto the children of men" [2 Nephi 27:13]. [In the Introduction to The Book of Mormon, the following eight men also testify that they saw the gold plates: Christian Whitmer, Jacob Whitmer, Peter Whitmer, Jr., John Whitmer, Hiram Page, Joseph Smith, Sen., Hyrum Smith and Samuel H. Smith.] The unlearned man [**Joseph Smith, Jr.** (Supplement C)] will be instructed to take the words which are not sealed and deliver them to another "that he may show them unto the learned, saying 'Read this, I pray thee.'" The learned man will ask to have the book [the gold plates] brought to him saying he will then read them. The learned man will be interested in material gain, not in the glory of the Lord. He will be told, "I cannot bring the book, for it is sealed." The learned man will reply, "I cannot read it." The Lord will again deliver the book [the gold plates] to the unlearned man [Joseph Smith, Jr.] and he shall read them. The unlearned man will say that he is unlearned. The Lord will tell him that the learned have rejected his words but "I am able to do mine own work; wherefore thou shalt read the words which I shall give unto thee" [v. 20]. The unlearned man will be commanded to not touch the part that is sealed for the Lord will bring that part forth in his own due time. After the unlearned man has read the words the Lord wants him to read and obtained the witnesses, the book will again be hidden up unto the Lord. The Lord will bring forth a marvelous work and a wonder in the latter days [2 Nephi 27].

There will be many false churches built up in the latter days, and apostasy shall abound [2 Nephi 28].

Many Gentiles will reject the Lord's words to the Nephites [The Book of Mormon] saying, "A Bible! A Bible! We have got a Bible, and there cannot be any more Bible" [2 Nephi 29:3]. The Bible comes from the Jews, written to the Gentiles for their salvation, and few acknowledge their diligent efforts. Instead, they have persecuted the Jews [vs. 4-5]. God has revealed his word to people in other nations, too, and more records have been kept which will someday come forth. The testimony of two nations is a witness that God is God. The world will be judged out of the books the Lord has caused to be written [2 Nephi 29:11].

The Gentiles will carry the words that have been written to the remnant of Nephi's[1] seed. The Gospel of Jesus Christ shall be declared among them, and they will be restored unto the knowledge of their fathers and to the knowledge of Jesus Christ, which knowledge was had among their fathers. They shall become a pure and delight some people again. The scattered Jews shall begin to believe in Christ and shall be gathered together. The wicked shall be destroyed. Satan shall be bound for a time [2 Nephi 30].

143. LORD, JESUS CHRIST, SAVIOR, REDEEMER, MESSIAH

1 Nephi 1:1. Long before the Savior's visit to **Lehi's**[1] (#1) descendants in America, 600 years after Lehi[1] and his family left Jerusalem, they knew he would come. They were aware of events that would surround his birth, his ministry, and his death. [See 1 Nephi 10:4-11.] They worshipped him as their Lord, and looked forward to his coming as the promised Messiah. There are many references made to him prior to his actual appearance among these people following his death and resurrection. [See the Index to The Book of Mormon.] They even knew he would be called Jesus Christ [2 Nephi 25:16] and that his mother would be a virgin named **Mary** (SA #25) [Mosiah 3:8]. The events that took place during his visit here in the Americas follow in the appropriate chronological place. [See #143.]

7. LABAN

1 Nephi 3:3. <u>LABAN</u> had possession of the record of the Jews which was written upon plates of brass.

The Lord told **Lehi**[1] (#1) to send his sons back to Jerusalem to obtain the plates. When **Laman**[1] (#3) went to Laban to ask for them, Laban thrust him out and sent his servants to slay him. When the four brothers returned with their gold and silver and offered to give it all to him in return for the brass plates, he again became angry and thrust them out and sent his servants to slay them. Meanwhile, an angel of the Lord interceded in behalf of Sam (#5) and **Nephi**[1] (#6) as they were being beaten by Laman[1] and **Lemuel** (#4) and told them to return once more to Laban and that the Lord would deliver him into their hands. When they returned this time, Nephi[1] found him lying drunken on the ground. The Spirit constrained him to slay Laban, indicating that it is better for one man to perish than for a nation to dwindle and perish in unbelief. Therefore, Nephi[1] smote off Laban's head with Laban's own sword. Nephi[1] then obtained the plates.

1 Nephi 5. Laban and Lehi[1] were descendants of **Joseph**[1] (SA #7), even that Joseph who was sold into Egypt, the son of **Jacob**[1] (SA #8). That is why Laban and his fathers had kept the records.

8. ZORAM[1]

1 Nephi 4:20. <u>ZORAM</u>[1] was **Laban's** (#7) servant. [**Zoram**[2] (#71) was a Nephite chief captain. **Zoram**[3] (#90) was a Nephite apostate.] Zoram[1] gave the brass plates to **Nephi**[1] (#6), who was disguised as Laban after beheading him, and then accompanied Nephi[1] to his brethren outside the city wall. When Zoram[1] discovered he had been deceived, he was frightened, but Nephi[1] restrained him. He and his brothers told him he would be a free man if he would go into the wilderness with them, which he did.

1 Nephi 16:7. Zoram[1] married Ishmael's[1] (#9) oldest daughter. Nephi[1] and his brothers married the other daughters.

9. ISHMAEL[1]

1 Nephi 7:2. <u>ISHMAEL</u>[1] was an Ephraimite from Jerusalem [c. 600 B.C.]. [**Ishmael**[2] (#66) was the grandfather of **Amulek** (#64).] [*Note:* There is another Ishmael in the Old Testament, **Abraham's** (SA #16) first son by Hagar, **Sarah's** (SA #17) handmaiden. However, he is not listed in the Index to The Book of Mormon and, therefore, has no super-script number affixed to his name. Were he given a superscript number, he would be Ishmael[1] ; Ishmael[1] would then be Ishmael[2]; and Ishmael[2] would be Ishmael[3].] **Nephi**[1] (#6) and his brothers persuaded Ishmael's[1] family to join their family in the wilderness. Ishmael[1] had at least two sons and probably five daughters. His sons were already married. His sons and their families, and two of his daughters, along with **Laman**[1](#3) and **Lemuel** (#4), rebelled against Nephi[1] , Sam (#5), Ishmael[1] and his wife as they traveled in the wilderness. They bound Nephi[1] and planned to take his life. The Lord loosed Nephi's[1] bands.

Laman[1] and Lemuel sought to lay hands upon Nephi[1] again, but Ishmael's[1] wife, a daughter, and one of his sons pleaded with Laman[1] and Lemuel, and their hearts were softened.

1 Nephi 16:7. His eldest daughter eventually married Zoram[1] (#8). His other daughters married Nephi[1] and his brothers.

1 Nephi 16:34. Ishmael[1] died and was buried in the place they called Nahom as they traveled in the wilderness. His daughters mourned his loss and complained against Lehi[1] (#1) and Nephi[1].

10.* JACOB[1]

1 Nephi 18:7. **JACOB**[2] was **Lehi's**[1] (#1) and **Sariah's** (#2) firstborn in the wilderness. **[Jacob**[1] (SA #8) was the father of the twelve tribes. His name was changed to Israel. He lived approximately 1800 B.C. **Jacob**[3] (#109) and Jacob[4] (#142) were apostate Nephites.]

2 Nephi 5. When **Nephi**[1] (#6) and the people fled to prevent Nephi[1] from getting killed by **Laman**[1] (#3) and **Lemuel** (#4) and their supporters, Jacob[2] went with them. He was consecrated by Nephi[1] to be a priest and teacher over the Nephites.

2 Nephi 6. Jacob[2] spoke to the people and spoke of things which are, and which are to come, and read to them the words of **Isaiah**[1] (SA #11). He recounted Jewish history and indicated that the Lord had shown unto him that the people in Jerusalem had been carried away. The Lord had also shown unto him that they would return again. The angel who spoke to Jacob[2] had also taught him that the Lord God would manifest himself in the flesh, be scourged and crucified. Therefore, the Jewish people would be smitten and afflicted and driven to and fro. When the people come to a knowledge of their Redeemer, they will be gathered together again to the lands of their inheritance. The Gentiles will assist in bringing this to pass. The Messiah will come in power and glory when he comes the second time [v. 14] to redeem his people.

2 Nephi 9. Jacob[2] continued his exhortation to his brethren. He again reminded them that the Jews would eventually be restored to their lands of promise. He taught them regarding the atonement of **Christ** (#143) and that the atonement ransoms man from the fall. He taught that the bodies of the dead shall come forth from the grave and their spirits shall come forth from hell and from paradise and be reunited in the resurrection. Everyone will have to stand before the judgment seat of God: those who are righteous will be righteous still, and those who are filthy will be filthy still. The righteous shall be saved in the kingdom of God. He outlined the consequences of sin, and he taught that the Holy One of Israel is the keeper of the gate and he cannot be deceived; no unclean thing will be allowed to pass through the gate.

2 Nephi 10. Jacob[2] reminded his people that the Lord had promised that their seed would not be completely destroyed, but that in future generations a righteous branch would come forth, and the promises of the Lord would be fulfilled. An angel told Jacob[2] that the Redeemer's name would be Christ. Christ would come among the Jews and be crucified by them. When the Jews accept Christ as the Redeemer, they will once more be restored to their lands. America would be a land of liberty unto the Gentiles and there would be no kings or queens upon this land. The Lord will fortify it against all other nations. Those that fight against Zion shall perish. The Gentiles who do not rebel against the Lord will be numbered among the house of Israel. Other isles of the sea are also inhabited by members of the house of Israel. We have free agency to choose the way of everlasting death or the way of eternal life; therefore, we should reconcile ourselves to the way of God.

2 Nephi 11:3. Jacob[2] indicated that he, like Isaiah[1] and Nephi[1], had seen the Redeemer.

Jacob 1. Prior to Nephi's[1] death, he gave the records to Jacob[2]. Nephi[1] had consecrated Jacob[2] and Joseph[2] (#11) to be priests and teachers of their people. Under the reign of the second king, the people began to grow in wickedness.

Jacob 2. Jacob[2] admonished the people against setting their hearts upon riches and warned them against the sin of pride. He encouraged them to share with their brethren, that all might be rich. He counseled them to seek the kingdom of God first, before seeking riches. God delights in the chastity of women. Unauthorized plural marriage is condemned by God.

Jacob 3. Jacob[2] continued to admonish his people, reminding them that the **Lamanites** (#12) were being faithful to the commandment to have only one wife and no concubines. He warned them against fornication, lasciviousness, and every kind of sin. He told them of the consequences of sin.

Jacob 4. Jacob[2] reminded his people that all of the holy prophets, including those of the Old Testament, worshiped the Father in the name of Christ. **Abraham's** (SA #16) offering of **Isaac** (SA #9) was a similitude of God and his Only Begotten Son. Don't seek to counsel God, but take counsel from him and be reconciled unto him. Jacob[2] said, "The Spirit speaketh the truth and lieth not." The Jews sought for things they could not understand. "Blindness" comes by looking beyond the mark. Jacob[2] prophesied that the Jews would reject the foundation stone.

Jacob 5. Jacob[2] reminded his people of the prophet **Zenos's** (SA #14) allegory of the olive tree, which Zenos likened unto the house of Israel.

Jacob 6. Jacob[2] prophesied that the prophecies of Zenos, wherein he likened the house of Israel to an olive tree, would surely come to pass. After Israel is gathered in the last days, the world will be burned with fire. The wicked shall be cast away into the lake of fire and brimstone; the righteous shall obtain eternal life.

Jacob 7:1-20. When Sherem (#19) came denouncing the fact that Christ would ever exist, Jacob[2] confounded him in all his words. When Sherem asked for a sign, Jacob[2] left it up to God whether or not to smite him. Sherem was smitten and had to be nourished for several days. Shortly before his death, Sherem spoke to the people and confessed he was wrong.

Jacob 7:27. Prior to Jacob's[2] death, he passed the records on to his son **Enos**[2] (#20).

Alma 3:6. We are reminded by later prophets that Nephi[1], Jacob[2], Joseph[2] and **Sam** (#5) were just and holy men.

11. JOSEPH[2]

1 Nephi 18:7. <u>JOSEPH</u>[2], the son of **Lehi**[1] (#1), was his secondborn in the wilderness. [**Joseph**[1] (SA #7) was the son of **Jacob**[1] (SA #8). He had the coat of many colors and was sold as a slave into Egypt. His story is recorded in the Old Testament.]

2 Nephi 5. When **Nephi**[1] (#6) and the people fled to prevent Nephi[1] from getting killed by **Laman**[1] (#3) and **Lemuel** (#4) and their followers, Joseph[2] and his family went with them. Nephi[1] consecrated Joseph[2] to be a priest and teacher over the Nephites.

Alma 3:6. We are told that Nephi[1], Joseph[2], **Jacob**[2] (#10) and **Sam** (#5) were just and holy men.

2
People First Mentioned in the Book of 2 Nephi

12. LAMANITES

2 Nephi 5:14. **LAMANITES** were the descendants of **Laman**[1] (#3). Eventually, everyone who rebelled against **Nephi**[1] (#6) and the Lord, and aligned themselves with this group, were called Lamanites. The Lamanites and **Nephites** (#13) battled throughout the 1000 years covered by The Book of Mormon. Periodically, the Lamanites became more righteous than the Nephites. Between 90-77 B.C., a group of Lamanites became converted to the gospel and joined the Nephites, taking upon themselves the name of **Anti-Nephi-Lehies** (#84). By the end of the 62nd year of the judges, the more part of the Lamanites had become a righteous people, more so than the Nephites. The Lamanites destroyed the Nephites in the final great battle around A.D. 385. [The American Indians are descendants of the remnants of the Lamanites.]

3

People First Mentioned in the Book of Jacob

13. NEPHITES

Jacob 1:13. <u>**NEPHITES**</u> were the descendants of **Nephi**[1] (#6) and his followers. Eventually, all those who accepted the gospel and joined with the followers of Nephi[1] were called Nephites. The Nephites and the **Lamanites** (#12) battled each other throughout the 1000 years covered by The Book of Mormon. Due to the Nephites' wickedness as they turned away from the Lord, the Lamanites were allowed to destroy them in the final great battle around A.D. 385.

14. JACOBITES

Jacob 1:13. <u>**JACOBITES**</u> were descendants of **Jacob**[2] (#10). They were included among the Nephites (#13).

15. JOSEPHITES

Jacob 1:13. <u>**JOSEPHITES**</u> were the descendants of **Joseph**[2] (#11). They were included among the **Nephites** (#13).

16. ZORAMITES[1]

Jacob 1:13. The early <u>**ZORAMITES**</u>[1] were descendants of Zoram[1] (#8) and joined with the Nephites (#13). The later Zoramites[2] (#89) were apostate Nephites, followers of **Zoram**[3] (#90).

4 Nephi 1. These Zoramites were descendants of the earlier, righteous Zoramites, and were true believers in Christ [v. 37].

17. LEMUELITES

Jacob 1:13. **LEMUELITES** were descendants of Lemuel (#4). They rebelled against Nephi[1] (#6) and the Lord and aligned themselves with the Lamanites (#12).

18. ISHMAELITES

Jacob 1:13. **ISHMAELITES** were descendants of **Ishmael**[1] (#9).

Alma 4. They united with the **Lamanites** (#12) and willfully rejected the gospel [v. 7].

19. SHEREM

Jacob 7:1-20. **SHEREM** denied that Christ would ever be. He contended with **Jacob**[2] (#10) and asked for a sign. He drew many people away. However, he was given a sign; he fell to the earth and had to be nourished for several days. He asked Jacob[2] to call the people together because he was about to die and wanted to speak to them. He confessed he was wrong before he died.

20.* ENOS[2]

Jacob 7:27. **ENOS**[2], the son of **Jacob**[2] (#10), received the records from his father shortly before Jacob's[2] death. [**Enos**[1] (SB #2) was the grandson of **Adam** (SA #4). No mention is made of him in The Book of Mormon.]

Enos 1. Enos[2] wrote one chapter consisting of 27 verses while he had the records. In those verses, he recounted that, as he prayed to his Maker, a voice came unto him declaring that his sins were forgiven and that he would be blessed. He spent the remainder of his life preaching among the **Nephites** (#13) and trying to convert the **Lamanites** (#12). He pleaded with the Lord that the records would be preserved and eventually be brought forth unto the Lamanites. He died approximately 420 B.C., 179 years after **Lehi**[1] (#1) and his family left Jerusalem. The records were given to his son **Jarom** (#21) to keep.

4

People First Mentioned in the Book of Jarom

21.* JAROM

Jarom 1:1. <u>JAROM</u> was the son of **Enos**[2] (#20). He kept the record after Enos[2] died. Because the plates were small, he declined to record his prophecies or revelations, indicating that his fathers had already written of the same things. He kept the records for 59 years and recorded one chapter consisting of 15 verses. He indicated that there were many battles with the **Lamanites** (#12), but the Nephite kings and leaders were righteous and taught the people so they were able to withstand the Lamanites. He mentioned the kinds of things the **Nephites** (#13) excelled in doing: they fortified their cities, multiplied exceedingly, became very rich in gold and silver and precious things; they excelled in workmanship of wood, in buildings, and in machinery, among other things. He also indicated that there were many prophets. Two hundred and thirty-eight years had passed away since **Lehi**[1] (#1) left Jerusalem, and Jarom passed the record on to his son **Omni** (#22).

22.* OMNI

Jarom 1:15. <u>OMNI</u> was the son of **Jarom** (#21). He received the plates from his father and was told to keep the records [361 B.C.] He said that he, himself, had not kept the statutes and commandments of God as he should have, and had been a wicked man. He recorded three verses of scripture [Omni 1:1-3] during the 44 years he had the records. He passed the record on to his son **Amaron** (#23). [It was now 317 B.C.; 282 years had passed away.]

5

People First Mentioned in the Book of Omni

23.* AMARON

Omni 1:3. <u>AMARON</u> was the son of **Omni** (#22). He recorded that by the time 320 years had passed away, the more wicked part of the Nephites were destroyed. He recorded five verses of scripture and passed the record on to his brother **Chemish** (#24).

24.* CHEMISH

Omni 1:8. <u>CHEMISH</u> was the son of **Omni** (#22) and the brother of **Amaron** (#23). He recorded only one verse of scripture and then passed the record on to his son **Abinadom** (#25).

25.* ABINADOM

Omni 1:10. <u>ABINADOM</u> was the son of **Chemish** (#24). He wrote just two verses of scripture indicating that there had been many wars and much contention between the **Nephites** (#13) and **Lamanites** (#12) and that he knew of no new revelations nor new prophecies so he felt that what had previously been recorded was sufficient. The secular record, he said, was engraven upon plates had by the kings.

26.* AMALEKI[1]

Omni 1:12. <u>AMALEKI</u>[1], the son of **Abinadom** (#25), was born in the days of **Mosiah**[1] (#27), king over the land of Zarahemla. Amaleki[1] lived to see his death [v. 23]. [**Amaleki**[2] (#36) was part of the expedition group that sought **Zeniff's** (#31) group.] **King Benjamin** (#30) reigned in Mosiah's[1] stead [279 B.C. to 130 B.C.]. Amaleki[1] recorded just 14 verses. In those few verses, he told a little about Mosiah[1] and the group of people found in the land of Zarahemla. He also mentioned the Jaredite record. [The people mentioned in the Jaredite record begin with #179.] He had no seed so he passed the record on to King Benjamin because he knew him to be a just man before the Lord.

27. MOSIAH[1]

Omni 1:12. MOSIAH[1] was a Nephite prophet and king in Zarahemla and the father of **Benjamin** (#30). [**Mosiah**[2] (#32) was a Nephite king and son of Benjamin.] Mosiah[1] was warned by the Lord to flee out of the land of Nephi. He took the believers with him. They were led to a land called Zarahemla. The land was already occupied by a people who had come out of Jerusalem when king **Zedekiah**[1] (SA #1) was carried away captive into Babylon. Mosiah[1] was made king over the land of Zarahemla; he had the people of Zarahemla taught in his language. Mosiah[1] interpreted engravings containing an account of **Coriantumr**[2] (#232).

28. PEOPLE OF ZARAHEMLA

Omni 1:14. The PEOPLE OF ZARAHEMLA were a people king **Mosiah**[1] (#27) and his people discovered living in Zarahemla when they fled from the land of Nephi. These people came out from Jerusalem at the time that **Zedekiah**[1] (SA #1), king of Judah, was carried away captive into Babylon. They had journeyed in the wilderness and had been brought across the great waters by the hand of the Lord. By the time Mosiah[1] discovered them, their language had become corrupted, they denied their Creator, and no one could understand them. Mosiah[1] caused that they should be taught in his language, after which **Zarahemla** (#29) gave a genealogy of his fathers. The people of Zarahemla and the people of Mosiah[1] united with Mosiah[1] as king [v. 9]. **Benjamin**, Mosiah's[1] son, (#30) reigned as king of this united group after his father.

Mosiah 1. When king Benjamin grew old, he called the people of Zarahemla and the people of Mosiah[1] together and proclaimed his son **Mosiah**[2] (#32) king [v. 10].

Mosiah 25. By about 120 B.C., when king Mosiah[2] gathered the combined group of people together, there were more descendants of Zarahemla than there were of **Nephi**[1] (#6). [But there were more than twice as many **Lamanites** (#12) as **Nephites** (#13) and the people of Zarahemla combined.]

Alma 22. When the people of Zarahemla first landed, the place they discovered was a land covered with bones, having been peopled at some former time, and they called it Desolation [v. 30].

29. ZARAHEMLA

Omni 1:14. ZARAHEMLA was a descendant of **Mulek** (#49) [Mosiah 25:2]. He rejoiced exceedingly when he and his people were discovered by king **Mosiah**[1] (#27) and his followers. His ancestors had come out of Jerusalem at the time that **Zedekiah**[1] (SA #1), king of Judah, was carried captive into Babylon. After learning the language of Mosiah[1], he gave a genealogy of his fathers according to his memory. He and his people united with Mosiah[1] and his followers.

Mosiah 7:3. **Ammon**[1] (#35) was a descendant of Zarahemla.

Helaman 1:15. **Coriantumr**[3] (#123) was a descendant of Zarahemla.

179. JAREDITES

Omni 1:21-22. The JAREDITES are mentioned here in the Book of Omni because this is an abridged account which **Mormon**[2] (#159) abridged centuries later. Thus, when he made his abridgment, he had read their record. However, because their history appears in The Book of Mormon later on, their record begins with #179. Suffice it to say at this point that they came out from the tower at the time the Lord confounded the language of the people. However, he did not confound the language of the Jaredites. **Mosiah**[1] (#27) interpreted engravings that gave an account of **Coriantumr**[2] (#232) and the Jaredite people.

232. CORIANTUMR[2]

Omni 1:21. <u>CORIANTUMR</u>[2]**,** a **Jaredite** (#179), was discovered by the **people of Zarahemla** (#28); and he dwelt with them for the space of nine moons. His first parents came out from the tower at the time the Lord confounded the language of the people. [See the Jaredite record, which begins with #179.] While Coriantumr[2] is mentioned in the Book of Omni, his history doesn't appear until later in The Book of Mormon. His record follows in its proper sequence, #232. [**Coriantumr**[1] (#197) was an early Jaredite; **Coriantumr**[3] (#123) was an apostate Nephite who commanded the Lamanite forces.]

30.* KING BENJAMIN

Omni 1:23. <u>KING</u> <u>BENJAMIN</u> was a Nephite prophet king, the son of **Mosiah**[1] (#27). He kept the records after **Amaleki**[1] (#26) and was a holy man who reigned over his people in righteousness.

Mosiah 2. He labored with his own hands so that he might serve the people and they would not be laden with taxes [v. 14]. He had his son **Mosiah**[2] (#32) call all the people together so he could declare Mosiah[2] to be the next king and to give them a name. The people pitched their tents and assembled by families. Because the multitude was so large, king Benjamin built a tower so the people could hear him. He also had his words written down and distributed to those who could not hear him. He taught the people about service, that "when ye are in the service of your fellow beings, ye are only in the service of your God," and he cautioned them about the sorry state of those who fall away and the blessed state of those who remain faithful.

Mosiah 3. An angel of the Lord appeared to King Benjamin and instructed him regarding the birth, life, mission, death and resurrection of **Jesus Christ** (#143), "and his mother shall be called **Mary**" (SA #25) [v. 8]. Salvation will come through no other name, only through **Jesus Christ**.

Mosiah 5. He instructed his people to take upon themselves the name of Christ [v. 8].

Mosiah 6. King Benjamin kept a record of the names of all the people who had entered into a covenant with God to keep his commandments. He consecrated his son Mosiah[2] to be a ruler and king over the people. He also appointed priests to teach the people. He died about 121 B.C.

Words of Mormon 1:18. King Benjamin and the prophets labored to establish peace in the land following battles with the **Lamanites** and by getting rid of contention, dissensions, false prophets and false priests.

31. ZENIFF

Omni 1:28. <u>**ZENIFF**</u> may or may not be the man **Amaleki**[1] (#26) described as "a strong and mighty man, a stiffnecked man" who initially led the group of people seeking to return to the land of Nephi. However, he was with them, and he said he contended with my brethren in the wilderness [Mosiah 9:2]. In the battle that erupted, all but 50 members of this group were slain. After the survivors returned to Zarahemla, another group was gathered (Omni 1:29), and Zeniff did lead this group of people out of Zarahemla around 200 B.C. to return to the land of Nephi, as he was over-zealous to possess the land of their inheritance. Amaleki's[1] brother was one of the people who went with Zeniff. [Zeniff is not referred to by name until Mosiah 7:9].

Mosiah 7. It is the descendants of this group, living in the land of Nephi, that we hear about from **Ammon**[1] (#35).

Mosiah 9. King **Laman**[2] (#41), king of the Lamanites, covenanted with Zeniff that he and his people could possess the land of Lehi-Nephi and the land of Shilom. However, his purpose was to ultimately bring them into bondage. After 12 years, king Laman[2] grew uneasy. The two groups engaged in battle. Many people were killed: 3,043 **Lamanites** (#12) and 279 **Nephites** (#13) in one day and a night [v. 18].

Mosiah 10. For 22 years they inherited the land and the people were industrious. They had peace for many years. However, when king Laman[2] died, his son **Laman**[3] (#42) reigned in his stead. King Laman[3] came to war against Zeniff and his people. Zeniff grew old and conferred the kingdom on his son **Noah**[3] (#40), about 160 B.C.

6

People First Mentioned in The Words of Mormon

159.* MORMON²

Words of Mormon 1:1. **MORMON**² was born about A.D. 311 [See Mormon 1:15]. His father was also called **Mormon**¹ (#160). Mormon², a Nephite prophet, general, record keeper and abridger, abridged the large plates of Nephi. As he finished abridging the record, prior to giving the record to his son **Moroni**² (#162), he inserted some words. These words were written about A.D. 385 and are inserted out of chronological order. Mormon's² life and works appear in their proper sequence, #159. [Throughout various places in The Book of Mormon, Mormon² editorializes, interjects ideas and explains things in a condensed manner, indicating that the abridged record doesn't contain a hundredth of what there really was.]

162.* MORONI²

Words of Mormon 1:1. **MORONI**² was the son of **Mormon**² (#159) and was the last person to keep the records. He is mentioned here, but this is chronologically out of order. His record (#162) appears further on according to his actual appearance in The Book of Mormon. [**Moroni**¹ (#97) was a righteous Nephite military commander.]

7

People First Mentioned in the Book of Mosiah

32.* MOSIAH²

Mosiah 1:2. <u>MOSIAH</u>² was the son of king **Benjamin** (#30). He began his reign when he was in his 30th year. [Mosiah¹ (#27) was his grandfather, a prophet and king in Zarahemla.]

Mosiah 6. Mosiah² reigned as king after his father [124 B.C.]. This was 476 years after **Lehi**¹ (#1) left Jerusalem. He tilled the earth himself so as to not be a burden to his people. There was no contention for the space of three years.

Mosiah 7. About 121 B.C., king **Mosiah²** sent 16 of their strong men to inquire about **Zeniff's** (#31) group that had left Zarahemla to return to the land of Lehi-Nephi about 200 B.C. The leader of this group was **Ammon**¹ (#35), a descendant of **Zarahemla** (#29).

Mosiah 22. **Ammon**¹ led king **Limhi** (#39) and his people to freedom. They were welcomed by Mosiah². They gave their records, including the records that Limhi's people had found, to Mosiah².

Mosiah 25. Mosiah² read (and caused to be read) the records of Zeniff and his people. He also read the account of **Alma**¹ (#45) and his brethren.

Mosiah 27. Mosiah² sent a proclamation throughout the land declaring that non-believers could not persecute believers. There was to be an equality among all men. Four of Mosiah's² sons [**Ammon²** (#51), **Aaron³** (#52), **Omner** (#53), **Himni** (#54)], and **Alma²** (#50), the son of **Alma¹**, persecuted the Church until an angel called them to repentance.

From this time on they preached to the people. Mosiah's[2] sons spent 14 years preaching among the **Lamanites** (#12).

Mosiah 28. Mosiah[2] translated the Jaredite plates with the two seer stones. He passed the records on to Alma[2] to keep and maintain, along with the interpreters.

Mosiah 29. None of his sons would have the kingdom conferred upon them, so kings were replaced with judges [c. 91 B.C.]. Mosiah[2] stressed to the people that kings are not always righteous and can be the cause of much wickedness; righteous judges would be much better for the people. He also reminded them that "it is not common that the voice of the people desireth anything contrary to that which is right; but it is common for the lesser part of the people to desire that which is not right . . . And if the time comes that the voice of the people doth choose iniquity, then is the time that the judgments of God will come upon you . . ." [vs. 26-27]. Alma[2] was appointed first chief judge. Mosiah[2] reigned for 33 years and died at the age of 63.

33. HELORUM

Mosiah 1:2. <u>**HELORUM**</u> was one of three sons of king **Benjamin** (#30) and brother of **Mosiah**[2] (#32).

34. HELAMAN[1]

Mosiah 1:2. <u>**HELAMAN**</u>[1] was one of three sons of king **Benjamin** (#30) and brother of **Mosiah**[2] (#32). [**Helaman**[2] (#91) was a prophet, military commander, and the son of **Alma**[2] (#50); **Helaman**[3] (#118) was the son of Helaman[2], a record keeper and chief judge.]

35. AMMON[1]

Mosiah 7:3. <u>**AMMON**</u>[1] was a strong and mighty man, a descendant of **Zarahemla** (#29). Ammon[1] was appointed by Mosiah[2] to lead 16 strong men to the land of Lehi-Nephi [121 B.C.] to inquire about **Zeniff** (#31) and their brethren who had left Zarahemla about 79 years earlier.

[**Ammon**² (#51) was the son of **Mosiah**² (#32) and was a missionary to the **Lamanites** (#12).]

Mosiah 7. When they first reached the land of Nephi, they were taken captive for fear they were **priests of Noah**³ (#43). They were imprisoned for two days, after which they were brought before king **Limhi** (#39) and given a chance to speak. King Limhi was excited to learn that his brethren in Zarahemla were still alive.

Mosiah 8. King Limhi addressed his people, and then he had Ammon¹ teach the people about what had happened in Zarahemla since Zeniff and their ancestors departed from there. Ammon¹ also taught them the last words which king **Benjamin** (#30) had taught the people. He told king Limhi that king Mosiah² in Zarahemla could translate the records Limhi's people found in a land covered with bones. [This ancient record, the book of Ether, recounts the history of the Jaredites and begins with #179.]

Mosiah 21. Ammon¹ declined to baptize Limhi and his converted followers, as he considered himself an unworthy servant.

Mosiah 22. When king Limhi and his people escaped from the Lamanites, Ammon¹ and his brethren led them back to Zarahemla. They brought their records with them.

36. AMALEKI²

Mosiah 7:6. **AMALEKI²** and two companions accompanied **Ammon**¹(#35) into the land of Nephi where they were met by king **Limhi** (#39). They were taken captive by the guards and cast into prison for two days. They were then brought before the king again. [**Amaleki**¹ (#26) was a Nephite record keeper.]

37. HELEM

Mosiah 7:6. **HELEM** was one of **Ammon's**¹ (#35) three companions who accompanied him into the land of Nephi where they were met by king Limhi (#39). They were taken captive by the guards and cast into prison for two days. They were then brought before the king again.

38. HEM

Mosiah 7:6. <u>HEM</u> was one of **Ammon's**[1] (#35) three companions who accompanied him into the land of Nephi where they were met by king Limhi (#39). They were taken captive by the guards and cast into prison for two days. They were then brought before the king again.

39. KING LIMHI

Mosiah 7:9. <u>KING</u> <u>LIMHI</u> was king over the land of Lehi-Nephi. He and his people were the descendants of those who left Zarahemla with **Zeniff** (#31) about 200 B.C. He was the son of king **Noah**[3] (#40) and grandson of Zeniff.

Mosiah 7, 8, 21. When king Limhi learned that **Ammon**[1] (#35) and those with him were from Zarahemla, he was delighted and had Ammon[1] speak to the people and teach them about what had happened in Zarahemla since Zeniff and their ancestors departed from there. Ammon[1] also taught them the last words which king **Benjamin** (#30) had taught the people. King Limhi then told Ammon[1] of some gold plates his people had found. King Limhi told Ammon[1] that he had sent 43 of his people into the wilderness to find the land of Zarahemla but that they had returned not having found it. However, they had discovered a land covered with bones and had returned with a record that they found there [24 gold plates plus breastplates made of brass and copper] [8:9-10]. This record is contained in the book of Ether and is a history of the Jaredites. It begins with #179. They also returned with other items they had found: swords, etc. Ammon[1] told Limhi that he could not translate the plates but that **Mosiah**[2] (#32), king of Zarahemla, could translate the records.

Mosiah 9-22. These chapters contain Zeniff's history. [See Zeniff (#31), Noah[3] (#40), **Laman**[2] (#41) and **Laman**[3] (#42).]

Mosiah 19. When his father, king Noah[3], fled from before the Lamanite army, Limhi was one of those who was taken captive by the **Lamanites** (#12). He did not wish his father to be destroyed; nevertheless, he knew his father was wicked. He, himself, was a just man. The king of the Lamanites, Laman[2], made an oath with the Nephites that his people would not slay them. The kingdom was conferred upon Limhi. Limhi promised the king of the Lamanites that they would pay one-half of all they possessed to him and his people. Thus, they were in bondage to the Lamanites and were taxed with a heavy tax.

Mosiah 20. Laman³ became king after Laman² died [Mosiah 10:6]. He and his people came to battle against Limhi and his people because he thought they had abducted their daughters. King Laman³ was captured. Limhi pacified him and convinced him that it was the **priests of Noah³** (#43) who were hiding in the wilderness who did it. King Laman³ was returned to his people.

Mosiah 21. Eventually, persecution by some of the Lamanites began. The Lamanites had Limhi's people surrounded on every side. Limhi's people battled against the Lamanites three times but were defeated each time. There was great mourning and lamentation among the people. They finally humbled themselves before the Lord. They began to prosper by degrees. Still, Limhi dared not even go outside the walls of the city without his guards. They watched in hopes of capturing the wicked priests of Noah³. Thus was the situation of Limhi and his people when Ammon¹ and his companions found them about 121 B.C.

Limhi was converted by Ammon¹ and his companions. Limhi and many of his people desired to be baptized, but Ammon¹ declined to do it because he felt unworthy.

Mosiah 22. Limhi's people plotted how to escape from the Lamanite bondage. **Gideon** (#47) proposed a plan: he suggested they gather the people together, along with their herds and flocks, and then get the Lamanite guards who guarded the back wall drunk, even more drunken than usual. Then, when the guards fell into a drunken sleep, they could pass through the secret pass on the left of their camp and travel around the land of Shilom. This they did, and Ammon¹ and his companions led them back to Zarahemla where they joined Mosiah² and his people.

Mosiah 25:16-18. King Limhi and his people were baptized by **Alma¹** (#45) in Zarahemla.

40. NOAH³

Mosiah 7:9. **NOAH**³ was the son of **Zeniff** (#31) and the father of **Limhi** (#39). [**Noah**¹ was the patriarch at the time of the flood (SA #26). He is referred to in Alma 10:22, 3 Nephi 22:9, and Ether 6:7. **Noah²** (#190) was an early Jaredite king, son of **Corihor**¹ (#188), and his record is recorded in the book of Ether which begins with #179.]

Mosiah 11. The kingdom was conferred upon Noah³ prior to Zeniff's death. He ruled in wickedness and had many wives and concubines. He taxed the people heavily for his own use and that of his friends and associates: the priests and their many wives and concubines. He built many elegant and spacious buildings, including a spacious palace and throne. He also built a high tower near the temple and another on the hill north of the land Shilom. He planted vineyards and built wine-presses and became a wine-bibber, as did the people. The **Lamanites** (#12) began to come upon them. Noah³ and his people became proud over their victories. He rebelled against the prophet **Abinadi** (#44) and imprisoned him. He ordered him to be slain.

Mosiah 17. Noah³ had Abinadi put to death by fire. As the flames consumed him, Abinadi prophesied that Noah³ would die in a like manner.

Mosiah 17:3. He accused Alma¹ (#45) of sedition.

Mosiah 19. After Noah's³ army returned from unsuccessfully trying to find Alma¹ and his followers, a division developed among his people. **Gideon** (#47) opposed king Noah³ and swore to slay him, but Noah³ fled from before Gideon. Gideon pursued Noah³ to a high tower. As Gideon was preparing to slay him, Noah³ discovered and announced that the Lamanites were in their borders and begged Gideon to spare his life. Gideon consented. When the Lamanites came to battle, king Noah³ fled with his people. As the Lamanites pursued them, Noah³ commanded the men to leave their wives and children and flee. Some did, others did not. Those that stayed with their wives and daughters were captured and their lives were spared. They were returned to the land of Nephi, but they had to pay high taxes to the Lamanites. The men who left their wives and daughters and fled with Noah³ vowed to return and seek revenge if their wives and daughters had been killed. Noah³ didn't want them to return. In anger, they killed him by fire as prophesied by Abinadi.

41. LAMAN²

Mosiah 7:21. LAMAN² was a Lamanite king who entered into a contract with king **Zeniff** (#31) for the purpose of ultimately bringing him and his people into bondage. Prior to his death, he conferred the kingdom upon his son **Laman³** (#42). [**Laman¹** (#3) was the eldest son of **Lehi¹** (#1); **Laman⁴** (#111) was a Nephite soldier.]

42. LAMAN³

Mosiah 10:6. LAMAN³, the son of **Laman²** (#41), became king of the **Lamanites** (#12) after his father [c. 178 B.C.] [**Laman¹** (#3) was the eldest son of **Lehi¹** (#1); **Laman⁴** (#111) was a Nephite soldier.]

Mosiah 20. King Laman³ and his people came to battle against **Limhi** (#39) and his people because the Lamanites thought Limhi's people had abducted their daughters. Laman³ was captured by Limhi's people. Rather than slay him, Limhi pacified him, convincing him that it was the **priests of Noah³** (#43) who were hiding in the wilderness who took the Lamanite daughters. Limhi returned Laman³ to his people.

Mosiah 21. There was sporadic peace between Laman's³ people and Limhi and his people, but the Lamanites, who surrounded Limhi's people on all sides, eventually began to persecute them. Limhi and his people, following a plan proposed by **Gideon** (#47) and aided by **Ammon¹** (#35) and his companions, finally escaped from king Laman's³ bondage by getting the Lamanite guards drunk.

43. PRIESTS OF NOAH³

Mosiah 11:5. The PRIESTS OF NOAH³ were priests appointed by king Noah³ (#40) after he got rid of all the priests his father **Zeniff** (#31) had consecrated. These priests were lazy, idolatrous, and engaged in whoredoms. They had many wives and concubines. Initially, **Alma¹** (#45) was one of those people appointed by Noah³ to be a priest. Noah³ ornamented their seats with pure gold. The wickedness of Noah[3] and the priests caused the people to become lifted up in the pride of their own strength.

Mosiah 12. The priests met in council with Noah[3] regarding the prophet **Abinadi** (#44). They questioned Abinadi and tried to cross him, but Abinadi confounded them. Alma[1] recognized the truth of what Abinadi was saying and was cast out by Noah[3], who then sought his life.

Mosiah 17. The priests were commanded by Noah[3] to kill Abinadi. They bound and scourged him and burned him to death.

Mosiah 19. When the Lamanite army came upon the city, Noah[3] told his people to flee. He and his priests fled with them. They escaped into the wilderness. The **Lamanites** (#12) came upon those people who would not leave their wives and daughters as commanded by Noah[3]. They spared their lives because they were charmed by the beauty of their women. They said the people could possess the land on condition that they pay high taxes and if they would deliver king Noah[3] up to them. Many of the men who had obeyed Noah[3] and fled with him and his priests wanted to return to their wives and daughters. King Noah[3] told them no. They rose up against him and killed him by burning him to death, fulfilling Abinadi's prophecy. The priests barely escaped, or they would have been put to death with the king.

Mosiah 20. The priests were ashamed and afraid to return to the city of Nephi, so they abducted 24 of the Lamanite daughters as they gathered together to sing and dance and make merry.

Mosiah 21. King **Limhi** (#39) desired to punish the priests of Noah[3] for abducting the Lamanite daughters, causing his people to have trouble with the Lamanites. However, even though they looked for them, his people did not find them.

Mosiah 23. When the Lamanite soldiers who were chasing Limhi and his followers when they escaped stumbled upon the priests, those daughters who had been abducted but who were now the wives of the priests pleaded for their husbands. The priests joined the Lamanites and were appointed teachers over them. This group of Lamanites and apostate

Nephite priests discovered Alma[1] and his people in Helam and placed them in bondage.

Mosiah 24. The chief priest was **Amulon** (#48). He exercised authority over Alma[1] and his people. Eventually, the Lord led Alma[1] and the people out of bondage. While the Lamanites were overcome by a deep sleep, Alma[1] and the people escaped and, after twelve days' journey, arrived in Zarahemla and joined king **Mosiah**[1] (#27).

Alma 24. When the Lamanites, stirred up to battle by the **Amalekites** (#81) and the **Amulonites** (#82), came against their brethren, the **Anti-Nephi-Lehies** (#84), the Anti-Nephi-Lehies would not defend themselves and 1,005 of them were killed. As a result, more than a thousand Lamanites became converted. The Lamanites who were converted were actual descendants of **Laman**[1] (#3) and **Lemuel** (#4). Those Lamanites not converted included the **Amalekites** (#81) and the **Amulonites** (#82). They were those who were of the order of **Nehor**[2] (#55).

Alma 25. The Lamanites associated with Amulon and the priests of Noah[3] became even angrier with the Nephites. Several battles ensued. Among the Lamanites who were killed by the Nephites were almost all the seed of Amulon and his brethren, the priests of Noah[3] [v. 4]. Those not slain fled into the east wilderness and battled against the Lamanites who believed. The Lamanites rose up against this group and "began to hunt the seed of Amulon and his brethren and began to slay them" [v. 8], thus fulfilling the words of Abinadi who had told them that they would be driven and hunted and slain.

44. ABINADI

Mosiah 11:20. **ABINADI** was a Nephite prophet [c. 150 B.C.] who called king **Noah**[3] (#40) and his followers to repentance.

Mosiah 12. Because of rejection and persecution, he came among the **Nephite** (#13) subjects of king Noah[3] in disguise. He prophesied that the people would be smitten with sore afflictions, famine and pestilence, and "shall have burdens lashed upon their backs; and be driven before like a dumb ass" [v. 5] and that Noah[3] "shall be valued even as a garment in a hot furnace" [v. 10]. He prophesied their destruction if they would not repent. He was cast into prison.

Mosiah 13. He expounded the Ten Commandments and told Noah[3] and his **priests** (#43) of the atonement. Salvation does not come through the law of Moses. Abinadi was protected by divine power as he prophesied that whatever Noah[3] and his people did to him, it would be as a type and a shadow of things which would come [v. 10].

Mosiah 15. Abinadi continued to teach Noah[3] and his priests. "God himself shall come down among the children of men, and shall redeem his people. And because he dwelleth in flesh he shall be called the Son of God, and having subjected the flesh to the will of the Father, being the Father and the Son—the Father, because he was conceived by the power of God; and the Son, because of the flesh; thus becoming the Father and Son" [vs. 1-3]. He taught that God "shall be led, crucified, and slain, the flesh becoming subject even unto death, the will of the Son being swallowed up in the will of the Father. And thus God breaketh the bands of death, having gained the victory over death; giving the Son power to make intercession for the children of men" [vs. 7-8]. He also taught that the Lord took upon himself the iniquity of the world and redeemed the children of men, satisfying the demands of justice. He taught that "these are they for whom he has died . . ." : all who have heard the words of the prophets and hearkened unto them [v. 11]; all of the prophets who have or who shall yet come [v. 13]. The first resurrection shall include all of the prophets, "and all those that have believed in their words, or all those that have kept the commandments of God" [v. 22]. It shall also include those "that have died before Christ came, in their ignorance, not having salvation declared unto them" [v. 24]. "And little children also have eternal life" [v. 25]. He taught that the time would come when salvation would be declared to every nation, kindred, tongue and people.

Mosiah 16. Abinadi taught that the Lord cannot redeem those who deny God and die in their sins. Every nation, kindred, tongue and people shall see the salvation of the Lord and confess that his judgments are just. There is a resurrection. Men will be resurrected to endless life and happiness or unto endless damnation, depending upon their own works.

Mosiah 17. **Alma**[1] (#45) believed Abinadi and pleaded with king Noah[3] to let Abinadi leave in peace. The king was very angry and had his servants scourge Abinadi's skin with faggots and then burn him to death. As the flames scorched him, he prophesied that king Noah[3] would suffer the same pains that he was suffering [vs. 15-19]. He died about 148 B.C.

45. ALMA[1]

Mosiah 17:2. ALMA[1] was one of **Noah's**[3] (#40) **priests** (#43) when we initially learn of him. He was a descendant of **Nephi**[1] (#6). He recognized the truth spoken by **Abinadi** (#44) and pleaded for Abinadi's life. He was cast out by king Noah[3] who then sent his servants out to slay him, but they were unsuccessful. He recorded all the words which Abinadi had spoken. [**Alma**[2] (#50) was his son.]

Mosiah 18. He repented of his iniquities. He fled to a place called Mormon, which was in the borders of the land. Many people, 450 souls, gathered about. He organized the church and baptized people in the waters of Mormon [c. 147 B.C.]. One of the first baptized was **Helam** (#46). When he baptized Helam, he also baptized himself. After that, he did not bury himself in the water again. He baptized about 204 people at this time. Alma[1] ordained priests, one for every 50 people. He taught that the priests should labor with their own hands for their support and that one day in every week should be set aside for the Lord. He stressed that they should share their goods: those that had more should give more, etc. Alma[1] and the people were apprised that Noah's[3] armies were about upon them so they gathered all their possessions together and departed into the wilderness.

Mosiah 23. Alma[1] and his people, having been warned of the Lord to flee because Noah's[3] armies were almost upon them [Mosiah 18:34; 23:1], traveled eight days and established the city of Helam in the land called Helam. Alma[1] refused to be their king, saying, "If it were possible that ye could always have just men to be your kings it would be well for you to have a king . . . ." However, since they could not always count on having righteous men for their kings, and since wicked men lead them astray, it was best to not have a king [vs. 6-8]. He taught them to love their neighbor as themselves. He was their high priest and founder of their church. He consecrated each of their priests and teachers.

The Lamanite armies which had followed after the people of king **Limhi** (#39) stumbled upon Alma[1] and his people in Helam as they [the Lamanite army] were trying to find their way to Nephi. These Lamanite armies had found the priests of Noah[3], the chief priest being **Amulon** (#48). The **Lamanites** (#12) had spared the lives of the priests when the priests' wives, the Lamanite daughters whom they had abducted years earlier, pleaded for mercy. The priests then joined up with the Lamanites. Alma[1] showed them the way to Nephi, but instead of keeping their promise to grant Alma[1] and his followers their freedom, they placed guards around them. Amulon was placed as a tributary king over Alma[1] and his people.

Mosiah 24. Amulon persecuted Alma[1] and his people. He decreed that if Alma[1] and the people were caught praying they would be put to death. The Lord lightened the burdens which were laid upon Alma[1] and his brethren. The Lord promised to deliver Alma[1] and the people so they gathered their flocks and herds together, along with all their grain and possessions. The Lord caused a deep sleep to come over the Lamanites and the task-masters, and Alma[1] and his group escaped into the wilderness. After 12 days journey in the wilderness, they reached the land of Zarahemla [c. 120 B.C.].

Mosiah 25. Mosiah[2] (#32) had Alma[1] address the people. Then Alma[1] baptized king Limhi and his people. King Mosiah[2] let Alma[1] establish churches throughout all the land of Zarahemla. Each of the seven churches had its ordained priests and teachers.

Mosiah 26. There were many of the rising generation who did not understand the words of king **Benjamin** (#30) because they had been little children when they heard him speak. As a result, they were not converted to the Church. Many sinned and caused problems. They were brought before Alma[1] to be judged. Alma[1] sent them to Mosiah[2] to be judged, but Mosiah[2] returned them to Alma[1]. Alma[1] inquired of the Lord and was told that those who repented should be forgiven; those who did not should be punished according to the law of the land and their names removed from the records of the Church.

Mosiah 27. Alma's[1] son **Alma**[2] (#50) and the sons of Mosiah[2] **[Ammon**[2] (#51), **Aaron**[3] (#52), **Omner** (#53) and **Himni** (#54)] were among the unbelievers and caused much dissension in the church and were a great hindrance to the prosperity of the church. However, after an angel spoke to them, they were converted and became great missionaries.

Alma 4. Alma[1] consecrated Alma[2] to be high priest over the church.

Mosiah 29:45. Alma[1] died at the age of 82 [c. 91 B.C.].

46. HELAM

Mosiah 18:12. **HELAM** was the first one to be baptized by **Alma**[1] (#45) in the waters of Mormon. Alma[1] buried himself also in the water this first time, but not thereafter [vs. 14-15].

47. GIDEON

Mosiah 19:4. **GIDEON** was one of king **Noah's**[3] (#40) people who opposed the king. He sought to kill the king but spared his life when Noah[3] announced that the **Lamanites** (#12) were approaching [v. 8]. He sent men into the wilderness secretly to search for Noah[3]. Gideon's men met the people who had fled, all except king Noah[3] and his **priests** (#43) [v. 18]. The people reported that when they had decided to return and face their fate, king Noah[3] forbade them, so they "caused that he should suffer, unto death by fire" [v. 20]. However, the priests had gotten away.

Mosiah 20. When the Lamanite daughters were abducted, Gideon, captain of king **Limhi's** (#39) army, reminded his king that Noah's[3] priests were still at large and were probably the ones who did it. Thus, king Limhi was able to persuade the Lamanite king, whom they had captured, that he and his people were not the guilty ones. The Lamanite king persuaded his people that Limhi and his people were not to blame, and they were pacified toward them.

Mosiah 22. Gideon advised king Limhi and **Ammon**[1] (#35) on a plan to escape from Lamanite bondage: get the Lamanite guards very drunk and escape through "the back pass, through the back wall, on the back side of the city" [v. 6]. They successfully escaped and journeyed to Zarahemla, led by Ammon[1] and his brethren.

Alma 1. In the first year of the judges [91 B.C.], **Nehor**[2] (#55), an apostate, came among the people preaching many false doctrines and leading many people away. Gideon, one of the teachers in the church, contended verbally with Nehor[2] over his false teachings. Nehor[2], in anger, slew Gideon who was now stricken with many years.

48. AMULON

Mosiah 23:32. **AMULON** was the leader of the **priests** (#43) of king **Noah**[3] (#40) who had escaped into the wilderness. He and his colleagues joined up with the Lamanites, who granted them their lives. They were traveling with them when they came upon **Alma**[1] (#45) and his people in Helam. Amulon was made a tributary king over Alma[1] and his people.

Mosiah 24. Amulon gained favor in the eyes of the Lamanite king, **Laman**[3] (#42), and he and his brethren were made teachers over the people. He persecuted Alma[1] and his followers and threatened them with death if they were caught praying to God. The Lord eventually caused a deep sleep to come upon Amulon's guards, and Alma[1] and his people escaped and returned to Zarahemla.

Alma 25. After the **Lamanites** (#12) killed 1,005 of their own brethren who had been converted and called themselves **Anti-Nephi-Lehies** (#84), they were angrier than ever with the **Nephites** (#13) and went to battle against them. They destroyed the people in Ammonihah and then had many more battles with the Nephites. Among the slain of the Lamanites were almost all the seed of Amulon and his brethren, who were the priests of Noah. The ones not killed escaped into the wilderness, "and having usurped the power and authority over the Lamanites, caused that many of the Lamanites should perish by fire because of their belief" [v. 5] inasmuch as many of them had been stirred up in remembrance of **Aaron's**[3] (#52) teachings. Because of the destruction to the Lamanites brought upon them by the remnant of the children of Amulon, who caused that the believers should be put to death by fire, many Lamanites rebelled and they began to hunt the seed of Amulon and his brethren. They slew those they captured, bringing to pass the words of the prophet, Abinadi. However, many of the Lamanites came over to the land of Ishmael and the land of Nephi and joined the Anti-Nephi-Lehies. They also buried their weapons of war.

49. MULEK

Mosiah 25:2. MULEK'S descendant was **Zarahemla** (#29).

Helaman 6. He was the son of the Jewish king **Zedekiah** (SA #1) [v. 10].

Helaman 8. All of his brothers were slain [v. 21].

50.* ALMA² (1)

Mosiah 27:8. ALMA² was the son of **Alma¹** (#45). When we first learn of him, he is a wicked and idolatrous man. He and the four sons of Mosiah² [**Ammon²** (#51), **Aaron³** (#52), **Omner** (#53) and **Himni** (#54)] are persecutors of the church. However, an angel of the Lord appeared to them and called them to repentance. Alma² became dumb and weak and had to be carried before his father. The priests fasted and prayed for two days, after which time he regained his strength and told of his repentance and redemption. From then on, he and the sons of Mosiah² went throughout the land confessing their sins and trying to repair the damage they had done earlier [v. 35].

Mosiah 28. He was given the records to keep and maintain, along with the interpreters [v. 20].

Mosiah 29. He was appointed to be the first chief judge. He was also the high priest, his father having conferred the office upon him. The reign of the judges commenced.

Alma 1. During the first year of the judges [91 B.C.], Alma² sentenced **Nehor²** (#55) to death for slaying **Gideon** (#47).

Alma 2. During the fifth year of the judges, he slew **Amlici** (#56) in battle.

Alma 4. During the sixth year of the judges, there was peace. During the seventh year of the judges, about 3,500 people were baptized. During the eighth year of the judges, the people began to be proud, and contentions developed in the church. During the ninth year of the judges [83 B.C.], Alma² conferred the office of chief judge upon **Nephihah** (#62) in order to devote full time to the ministry. Nevertheless, he retained the office of high priest.

Alma 5. Alma² preached that to gain salvation men must repent and keep the commandments, be born again, and do the works of righteousness. He taught that **Christ,** the **Good Shepherd** (#143), calls his people, and calls them by his name. Also, if a man does good works, he follows the voice of the Good Shepherd; if he does evil works, he follows the voice of the devil. He also taught that the names of the righteous shall be written in the book of life.

Alma 6. After Alma² finished speaking to the people in Zarahemla and the church was set in order, he went to preach in Gideon.

Alma 7. In Gideon, he rejoiced that the people had not fallen away like they had in Zarahemla. He told them that the coming of the **Redeemer** (#143) was not far away. The Redeemer would be born of **Mary** (SA #25), a virgin, in Jerusalem. He would go forth, suffering pains and afflictions and temptations of every kind, taking upon himself death that he may loose the bands of death, and taking upon himself the infirmities of his people. People must repent and be baptized and be born again or they cannot inherit the kingdom of heaven. Filthiness cannot be received into the kingdom of God. If the people have humility, faith, hope, and charity, they will always abound in good works.

Alma 8. Alma² returned to his home in Zarahemla for a while. At the beginning of the tenth year of the judges, Alma² traveled to Melek where he baptized many people. He then traveled three days on to Ammonihah where the people were not receptive to his teachings and reviled him. He left to go to the city of Aaron, but was met by an angel and told to return to Ammonihah. There he met and was befriended by **Amulek** (#64). They then traveled together to preach the gospel.

Alma 9. The people in Ammonihah continued to rebel against Alma². When he told them to repent or be destroyed, they tried to cast him into prison, but the Lord would not suffer it to be so at that time.

Alma 10. **Zeezrom** (#68), a lawyer in Ammonihah, accused Alma² and Amulek of preaching and reviling against their laws.

Alma 11. The Nephite monetary system is set forth. The lawyers tried to stir the people up so more lawsuits would be brought to them so they could get more money; therefore, they stirred the people up against Alma² and Amulek. Zeezrom tried to bribe Amulek into denying the existence of a Supreme Being. Amulek contended with him.

Alma 12. Then Alma² contended with Zeezrom. He explained things beyond that which Amulek explained: the mysteries of God can be given only to the faithful; men will be judged by their thoughts, beliefs, words and works, etc. He also discussed the plan of redemption and taught that this life is a probationary and preparatory state. Mercy comes through the Only Begotten Son. Zeezrom was converted.

Alma 13. Alma² taught that men are called as high priests and ordained after the manner of the order of God, and that they are called and pre-pared from the foundation of the world according to the foreknowledge of God and because of their exceeding faith and good works. Others were on the same standing with their brethren, but they hardened their hearts and, therefore, were not called as high priests. Alma² elaborated on the holy priesthood and the responsibility of high priests to teach the commandments. He referred to **Melchizedek** (SA #27) to whom **Abraham** (SA #16) paid tithes, and said there were others before and after him, but none greater than Melchizedek.

He stressed that angels of the Lord were declaring glad tidings through-out all the face of the earth, even to the peoples who were scattered, and that "angels are declaring it unto many at this time in our land; and this is for the purpose of preparing the hearts of the children of men to receive his word at the time of his coming in his glory" [v. 24].

Alma 14. Some people were converted, but the majority were not. Alma² and Amulek were bound and taken before their chief judge. The people testified against Alma² and Amulek. Zeezrom became very distraught, encircled about by the pains of his own guilt because of the blindness of the minds of the people which he had caused among them by his lying words. He tried to convince the people that he was guilty and that Alma² and Amulek were spotless before God. The people then reviled against him, too. The believers and their holy scriptures were burned by fire. The Lord constrained Alma² to not interfere. These martyrs would be received by the Lord in glory and their blood would stand as a witness against the people at the last day. Alma² and Amulek were cast into prison. They were mocked, hit and spat on. After many days, on the twelfth day of the tenth month in the tenth year of the judges, as the chief judge and people were mocking Alma² and Amulek, the cords binding Alma² and Amulek were broken. The people fell down in fear and could not flee. An earthquake caused the prison walls to collapse and everyone within the prison walls except Alma² and Amulek was killed.

Alma 15. Alma² and Amulek left Ammonihah and traveled to the land of Sidom. The people who had been cast out of Ammonihah because of their faith were gathered there. Zeezrom had also been kicked out. Because of the guilt he felt due to his wickedness, he lay sick with a burning fever in Sidom. He called for Alma² and Amulek to come to him. Alma² healed Zeezrom and then baptized him. He established the church in Sidom. Amulek left all of his riches for the gospel and was rejected by his friends, his father and his kindred. Therefore, Alma² took Amulek back to Zarahemla with him to his own house and administered unto him in his tribulations and strengthened him in the Lord.

Alma 16. On the fifth day of the second month of the eleventh year of the judges, the **Lamanites** (#12) came to battle against the **Nephites** (#13). The city of Ammonihah was destroyed and some people who lived around the borders of Noah were taken captive. **Zoram²** (#71), the chief captain of the Nephite armies, and his two sons, **Lehi²** (#72) and **Aha** (#73), inquired of Alma² where to go to rescue the Nephites who had been taken captive. Alma² inquired of the Lord and gave them directions. After Zoram² and his armies rescued their brethren, there was peace in the land for three years. Thus, the fourteenth year of the judges ended.

Alma 17. It was at this time that Alma², as he was traveling from Gideon to the land of Manti, met the sons of Mosiah as they traveled toward Zarahemla after their fourteen years of missionary work among the Lamanites.

Alma 17-26. [*Note:* These chapters do not talk about Alma², but tell of the missionary experiences of Mosiah's² sons: Ammon², Aaron³, Omner and Himni.]

Alma 27. At the conclusion of their fourteen years of missionary work, Alma² and the sons of Mosiah met each other as Alma² was on his way to Manti and the sons of Mosiah were on their way to Zarahemla. Alma² conducted his friends back to Zarahemla, even to his own house. Together they went and told the chief judge all that had happened to them during the past fourteen years. A survey was taken among the people to ascertain their desires regarding the **Anti-Nephi-Lehies** (#84). The people said they would welcome them and would give them the land of Jershon for an inheritance and that they would defend them in return for a portion of their substance to assist in maintaining the armies. Alma² returned with Ammon² into the wilderness to bring the converted Lamanites, the Anti-Nephi-Lehies, to Jershon.

Alma 28. During the fifteenth year of the judges, there were tremendous battles with the Lamanites, and many Lamanites and Nephites were slain. It was a time of mourning and great lamentation. And, thus, the fifteenth year ended.

Alma 29. Alma² wished that he could be an angel to cry repentance to all the world. However, he stated that the Lord grants unto all nations to have people from their own nation and tongue teach his word to them.

Alma 30. During the sixteenth year and the first part of the seventeenth year of the judges, there was peace throughout Zarahemla. In the latter part of the seventeenth year, **Korihor** (#86), a man who was Anti-Christ, preached against the prophecies concerning the coming of Christ and his atonement, and he led many people away.

Korihor went to Jershon, but the **people of Ammon**[2] (#84), the Anti-Nephi-Lehies, bound him up and carried him before Ammon[2], their high priest. He had Korihor carried out of the land.

Korihor then went to the land of Gideon and was taken before the high priest **Giddonah**[2] (#87). Giddonah[2] and the chief judge ordered him to be bound and taken to Zarahemla to be brought before Alma[2] and the chief judge who was governor over all the land. Korihor contended with Alma[2], implying that Alma[2] wanted the people to join the church so Alma[2] could get gain. Alma[2] reminded him he was paid nothing for preaching and that he worked with his own hands for his support. Korihor demanded a sign and was finally given one: he was struck dumb and, after confessing his wickedness, wandered from house to house, begging food for his support. His wanderings took him to the land of the **Zoramites**[2] (#89). As he went forth among them, he was run upon and trodden to death.

Alma 31. Alma[2] took Ammon[2], Aaron[3], Omner, Amulek, Zeezrom, and two of his own sons [**Shiblon** (#92) and **Corianton** (#93)] to preach to the **Zoramites**[2] (#89), who were apostate Nephites led by **Zoram**[3] (#90). [Himni was left in the church in Zarahemla.] When Alma[2] saw their perverse ways of worship, he cried unto the Lord, "O Lord God, how long wilt thou suffer that such wickedness and infidelity shall be among this people?" [v. 30]. After crying unto the Lord for strength for him and those with him, Alma[2] clapped his hands upon his missionary companions, and they were filled with the Holy Spirit. The group separated, going in different directions to teach the people.

Alma 32. Alma[2] and his brethren met with success in teaching the poor who were not allowed to worship in the synagogues and whose afflictions had humbled them. Faith and knowledge are not the same. If you have knowledge, you do not need faith. Alma[2] also taught that if a person has knowledge and falls away from the truth, his curse is greater than if he "only believeth, or only hath cause to believe, and falleth into transgression" [v. 19]. He compared the word unto a seed.

Alma 33. Alma[2] quoted **Zenos** (SA #14) and **Zenock** (SA #12) to illustrate that a person can pray and worship anywhere and that mercy is bestowed because of the Son. He also said that **Moses** (SA #2) had lifted up his staff in the wilderness so that those who looked on it would live. It was a type of the Son of God.

Alma 34. Amulek preached to the people.

Alma 35. Alma[2] and Amulek and their brethren finished preaching to the Zoramites[2] and went to the land of Jershon. The preaching of the word destroyed the craft of the Zoramites[2]. Thus, they expelled all of the converts. These converts then joined the people of Ammon[2], the Anti-Nephi-Lehies, in Jershon. The Zoramite ruler demanded that the people of Ammon[2] cast out the Zoramites[2] who had joined them. They refused, and the wicked Zoramites[2] joined with the Lamanites to wage war. This ended the seventeenth year of the judges.

The people of Ammon[2] gave up the land of Jershon to the Nephite armies and went to Melek. War commenced in the eighteenth year of the judges. Alma[2], Ammon[2], and Alma's[2] two sons returned to the land of Zarahemla. Alma[2] sorrowed because of the wickedness of the people.

Alma 36-42. Alma[2] called his sons together and gave commandments unto each one. Alma 36-37 contains Alma's[2] counsel to **Helaman[2]** (#91). Alma 38 contains Alma's[2] counsel to Shiblon. Alma 39-42 contains Alma's[2] reprimand and counsel to Corianton. Alma[2] then passed the records on to his son Helaman[2].

Alma 43-44. After Alma[2] gave his sons individual commandments, he and they preached among the people.

During the eighteenth year of the reign of the judges, the Nephites had to contend in battle with the Lamanites and the Zoramites[2] who became Lamanites. The leader of the Lamanites was **Zerahemnah** (#96); the leader of the Nephite armies was **Moroni[1]** (#97). Zerahemnah was willing to deliver up his weapons to Moroni[1], but he refused to promise that they would not come to battle again so Moroni[1] said they would end the conflict right then. When Zerahemnah rushed at Moroni[1] to slay him,

Lehi[3] (#98), one of **Moroni's**[1] soldiers, scalped him. Alma[2] concluded his record. Helaman[2] became the keeper of the record at this point, beginning with Alma 45.

Alma 45. In the nineteenth year of the reign of the judges, Alma[2] came to his son Helaman[2] and spoke to him. Alma[2] told Helaman[2] to record what he told him but to not make it known. He prophesied that the people would dwindle in unbelief 400 years from the time Jesus Christ manifests himself unto the Nephites. There would be wars, pestilences, famines and bloodshed until the Nephites became extinct. He then blessed Helaman[2] and his other sons, the earth for the righteous sake, and the church, and then "he departed out of the land of Zarahemla, as if to go into the land of Melek. And it came to pass that he was never heard of more; as to his death or burial we know not of . . . But behold, the scriptures saith the Lord took Moses unto himself; and we suppose that he has also received Alma[2] in the spirit unto himself; therefore, for this cause we know nothing concerning his death and burial" [vs. 18-19].

51. AMMON[2]

Mosiah 27:8, 34. **AMMON**[2] was one of the four sons of **Mosiah**[2] (#32). At first, he persecuted the church, but then he spent the rest of his life as a missionary after an angel appeared to him, his brothers, and their friend **Alma**[2] (#50). [**Ammon**[1] (#35) was the leader of an expedition to the land of Nephi that found **Limhi** (#39) and the descendants of **Zeniff** (#31).] Ammon[2] and his brothers all declined to become king after their father. As a result, kings were replaced with judges. About 92 B.C., Ammon[2] and his brothers [**Aaron**[3] (#52), **Omner** (#53) and **Himni** (#54)] traveled to the land of Nephi to preach to the **Lamanites** (#12). They spent fourteen years as missionaries to the Lamanites [c. 91- 77 B.C.]. At the end of this time, as they concluded their missionary labors with the Lamanites, they accidentally met up with Alma[2] as he was traveling to the land of Manti and they were headed to Zarahemla. They reported the happenings of the past fourteen years.

AMMON'S MISSIONARY EXPERIENCES
(Alma 17-26)

Alma 17. The brothers went their separate ways. Ammon[2] administered to each brother before they split up. Ammon[2] went to the land of Ishmael. He was taken captive and was bound. He was carried before king **Lamoni** (#74), a descendant of **Ishmael**[1] (#9). Ammon[2] told him he would like to dwell among them. Lamoni was pleased with Ammon[2] and wanted him to take one of his daughters to wife. Ammon[2] declined, but offered to be a servant. After three days, he went with the other servants to water the kings flocks at the waters of Sebus. The flocks were scattered by Lamanites who were there to water their flocks. The servants were terrified because King Lamoni had slain other servants for allowing their flocks to be scattered. Ammon[2] soothed their fears. They gathered their flock and protected them while Ammon[2] contended with the Lamanites. He slew some with stones, smote off arms with his sword, and slew their leader. They returned to the king with the flocks, carrying all the arms Ammon[2] had smitten off.

Alma 18. King Lamoni thought Ammon[2] was the Great Spirit. Ammon[2] fed the king's horses and then reported to him. He told him he was not the Great Spirit. Ammon[2] then taught Lamoni about God and everything contained in the scriptures even from the beginning. Lamoni believed Ammon[2] and fell to the earth as if dead. His servants carried him to his **wife** (#75). He lay there for two days and nights.

Alma 19. Lamoni received the light of everlasting life and saw the **Redeemer** (#143). Lamoni's wife sent for Ammon[2] and told him that some say that he stinketh . . . but as for myself, to me he doth not stink" [v. 5]. Ammon[2] awakened Lamoni, and Lamoni praised the Lord. Ammon[2], the king, the queen, and their servants all were overpowered with joy and sank to the earth. **Abish** (#76), a Lamanite woman who had been converted many years earlier, ran from house to house to tell the people what had happened. They gathered and murmured. One person, whose brother had been slain by Ammon[2] at the waters of Sebus while scattering the king's flocks, drew his sword to kill Ammon[2] but was struck by the Lord and fell dead. The converted woman servant was sorrowful as she witnessed the contention. She took the hand of the queen and the queen awoke. The queen was joyful and took King Lamoni by the hand and he awoke. When Ammon² awoke, he administered unto the people, as did Lamoni's servants.

Alma 20. Ammon² left the land of Ishmael and traveled to Middoni to deliver his brother Aaron³, **Muloki** (#77) and **Ammah** (#78) from prison. King Lamoni traveled with him because he said the king there, King **Antiomno** (#79), was a friend of his. On the way to Middoni, they ran into **Lamoni's father** (#80) who was king over all the land. He immediately commanded Lamoni to slay this **Nephite** (#13), Ammon². Lamoni refused. Lamoni's father drew his sword to slay Lamoni, but Ammon² stopped him. He tried to slay Ammon², but Ammon² withstood his blows and smote his arm so that he could not use it. Ammon² granted Lamoni's father his life in return for his promise that King Lamoni could retain his kingdom; that he not be angry with Lamoni; and that he allow Lamoni to do according to his own desires. Lamoni and Ammon² continued on to Middoni where they delivered Muloki, Ammah and Aaron³ from prison.

Alma 21. Ammon² and Lamoni returned from Middoni to the land of Ishmael. King Lamoni refused to allow Ammon² to serve him or to be his servant. Lamoni had synagogues built. He told his people they were a free people and were free to worship God according to their desires. Ammon² then taught the people all things pertaining to righteousness.

Alma 23. Those who were converted took upon themselves the name **Anti-Nephi-Lehies** (#84).

Alma 24. Ammon² and his brethren held a council with Lamoni and his brother, King **Anti-Nephi-Lehi** (#85), to determine how to defend themselves against Lamanite aggressors. They decided they would rather be slain by the Lamanite armies than take up the sword again. One thousand and five converted Lamanites were killed. Then many of the soldiers, seeing the people refuse to defend themselves, were converted so that more were converted than had died at the hands of their oppressors.

Alma 26. Ammon² rejoiced in the Lord. Aaron³ rebuked him because he thought he was being carried away unto boasting, but Ammon² said he was not boasting in his own strength but in the glory of God.

Alma 27. When the Lamanites, stirred up by the **Amalekites** (#81), continued to slay the people of Anti-Nephi-Lehi, Ammon² suggested they all journey down to the land of Zarahemla. The king was concerned that they would not be warmly welcomed because of their past murders. Ammon² said he would inquire of the Lord as to whether or not they should go to Zarahemla. They were directed to go to Zarahemla. Ammon² and his brethren went on ahead to see what kind of reception the Anti-Nephi-Lehies would receive from the people of Zarahemla. On the way, to their exceeding great joy, Ammon² and his brethren ran into their friend Alma² [v. 16; also Alma 17:1-2]. Ammon's² joy was so full that he fell to the ground, exhausted of his strength. The Anti-Nephi-Lehies were warmly welcomed and were given the land of Jershon. These people were then called "**the people of Ammon³**" or "**Ammonites**" (#84) by the **Nephites** (#13), and they were distinguished by that name ever after.

Note: This ends Ammon's² missionary experiences among the Lamanites.

Alma 28. After the people of Ammon² were established in the land of Jershon, the Lamanites waged another huge battle, the largest since **Lehi¹** (#1) had left Jerusalem. This was a time of great mourning and lamentation. The fifteenth year of the reign of the judges ended [76 B.C.] [v. 7].

Alma 30. Ammon² was made high priest over the people in Jershon, the Anti-Nephi-Lehies. When **Korihor** (#86), the Anti-Christ, came among the people preaching against the prophecies the prophets had spoken concerning the coming of **Christ** (#143), the people bound him and took him before Ammon². Ammon² banished Korihor and had him carried out of the land.

Alma 31. When Alma² received a report that the **Zoramites²** (#89) were perverting the ways of the Lord, he took a strong group of missionaries with him to Antionum to preach to the Zoramites². Ammon² went with

Alma². The missionaries all went their separate ways to preach and teach. The Lord provided for their needs in answer to Alma's² prayer of faith.

Alma 35. After preaching among the Zoramites², Ammon² and Alma², as well as the other missionaries, returned to Jershon. When the people of Ammon² went to Melek so the Nephite armies could fortify themselves in Jershon, Ammon² and Alma² and their brethren returned to Zarahemla.

52. AARON³

Mosiah 27:8, 34. <u>AARON³</u>, one of **Mosiah's²** (#32) four sons, initially persecuted the church. After an angel appeared to him, his brothers, and their friend **Alma²** (#50), he spent the rest of his life as a missionary after refusing to become king. [**Aaron¹** (SB #1) was the brother of **Moses** (SA #2) and is not referred to in The Book of Mormon; **Aaron²** (#219) was a Jaredite king.] Aaron³ and his brothers spent fourteen years as missionaries to the **Lamanites** (#12) [c. 91-77 B.C.]. At the end of the time with the Lamanites, he and his brothers accidentally met up with Alma² as he was traveling to the land of Manti and they were on their way to Zarahemla. They reported on the happenings of the past fourteen years [Alma 17-26].

AARON'S³ MISSIONARY EXPERIENCES
(Alma 21-26)

Alma 21. Aaron³ went to the land called Jerusalem. The Lamanites were hardened, but the **Amalekites** (#81) and the **Amulonites** (#82) were even harder, and they caused the Lamanites to harden their hearts even more. He taught in the synagogues, but the people contended against him, asking why angels do not appear unto them: "Are not this people as good as thy people?" [v. 5]. When he saw they would not listen to his words, he left Jerusalem and went to Ani-Anti. There he found **Muloki** (#77) and **Ammah** (#78) and his brethren. They contended with many there. When they found no one who would listen to them, then went to Middoni. Aaron³ and several of his brethren were cast into prison and the others fled into the surrounding regions. They suffered many things in prison. They were delivered by king **Lamoni** (#74) and **Ammon²** (#51).

Alma 22. After he departed out of the land of Middoni, he was led by the Spirit to the land of Nephi and to the house of **Lamoni's father** (#80), who was king over all the land. He bowed himself before the king and said, "Behold, O king, we are the brethren of Ammon², whom thou hast delivered out of prison" [v. 2]. He then said if the king would spare their lives, they would be his servants. The king refused to allow them to be his servants but said he would like them to administer unto him because he had been somewhat troubled in his mind because of the generosity and the greatness of the words of Ammon². He asked Aaron³ why Ammon² had not come up from Middoni. Aaron³ explained that the Lord had called him to go to Ishmael, to teach Lamoni's people. Aaron³ then taught the king about God [or the Great Spirit, as the king referred to him] and about all things from the creation and about the plan of redemption. The king believed and prostrated himself on the ground and was struck as if dead. When the **queen** (#83) saw her husband as if dead, she ordered her servants to slay Aaron³. They declined out of fear. She ordered them to call the people so they could slay Aaron³. Aaron³ stretched forth his hand and raised the king. The king then administered to all of his people as they assembled. The king ordered the people not to lay their hands on Ammon², Aaron³, **Omner** (#53) and **Himni** (#54) nor on any of their brethren.

Alma 23. The king granted Ammon³ and his brethren free access to the houses and temples of the Lamanites so they could preach. Thousands throughout the cities were brought to the knowledge of the Lord. None of those who were converted unto the Lord ever fell away, but they became a righteous people. They laid down their arms and vowed they would never fight again. Only one Amalekite was converted. No Amulonites were converted. The king desired to have a name whereby those who were converted might be distinguished from their brethren. After consulting with Aaron³ and the priests, they chose to be called **Anti-Nephi-Lehies** (#84).

Alma 24. The father of King Lamoni died shortly after bestowing the kingdom on one of his sons, whom he now called **Anti-Nephi-Lehi** (#85). This same year, the Lamanites made preparations for war against the Anti-Nephi-Lehies, who had sworn to never take up arms again. Therefore, Ammon² and all his brethren met in Midian and then traveled to Ishmael to hold a council with **Lamoni** (#74) and his brother Anti-Nephi-Lehi to decide what to do to defend themselves against the Lamanites. They decided they would rather perish than take up their swords again. One thousand and five converted Lamanites were slain by the Lamanite army, but more than that number of Lamanites were converted when they saw the people willingly die for their beliefs.

Alma 26. When Ammon² rejoiced in the Lord, Aaron³ rebuked him as he thought he was being carried away unto boasting. Ammon² said he was not boasting in his own strength but in the glory of God.

Alma 27. When the Lamanites, stirred up by the Amalekites, continued to slay the people of Anti-Nephi-Lehi, Ammon² suggested they all journey down to the land of Zarahemla. When the king was concerned that they would not be warmly welcomed because of their past murders, Ammon² said he would inquire of the Lord as to whether or not they should go to Zarahemla. They were directed to go to Zarahemla. Ammon², Aaron³ and their brethren went on ahead to see what kind of reception the Anti-Nephi-Lehies would receive from the people of Zarahemla. On the way, to their exceeding great joy, they encountered Alma² [v. 16; also Alma 17:1-2]. Ammon² was so full of joy that he fell to the ground, exhausted of his strength. Aaron³, Omner and Himni were also overjoyed to see Alma², but not so much as to exceed their strength. The Anti-Nephi-Lehies were warmly welcomed and were given the land of Jershon. These people were then called by the Nephites "**the people of Ammon²**" or "**Ammonites**" (#84), and were distinguished by that name ever after.

Alma 28. After the people of Ammon² were established in the land of Jershon, the Lamanites waged another huge battle, the largest since **Lehi¹** (#1) had left Jerusalem. This was a time of great mourning and lamentation. And the fifteenth year of the reign of the judges ended [v. 7]. It was now 76 B.C.

Note: This ends Aaron's³ missionary experiences among the Lamanites.

Alma 31. When Alma² received a report that the **Zoramites²** (#89) were perverting the ways of the Lord, he took a strong group of missionaries with him to Antionum to preach to the people. Aaron² went with Alma².

The missionaries went their separate ways to preach. The Lord provided for their needs in answer to Alma's[2] prayer of faith.

Alma 35. After preaching among the Zoramites[2], the missionaries [including Aaron[3] and Alma[2]] returned to Jershon. When the Ammonites left Jershon and went to Melek so the Nephite armies could use Jershon as a base camp, Aaron[3], Alma[2] and their brethren returned to Zarahemla.

53. OMNER

Mosiah 27:8, 34. <u>**OMNER**</u> was one of the four sons of **Mosiah**[2] (#32) who first persecuted the church. Then, after an angel appeared unto him, his brothers and **Alma**[2] (#50), he spent the rest of his life as a missionary.

Mosiah 28. He, like his brothers, refused to be king. He spent 14 years, along with his brothers, as a missionary to the **Lamanites** (#12) [c. 91-77 B.C.]. At the end of the time with the Lamanites, he and his brothers accidentally met up with Alma[2] as he was traveling to the land of Manti and they were on their way to Zarahemla. They reported on the happenings of the past 14 years.

Alma 17-26. These chapters explain Omner's and his brothers' missionary experiences. For details in this document regarding Omner's experiences, see **Aaron's**[3] (#52) Missionary Experiences [Alma 21-26]. Omner, **Himni** (#54) and Aaron[3] traveled together, but Aaron[3] seems to have been the leader of this group of missionaries.

Alma 31. Later, when Alma[2] received a report that the **Zoramites**[2] (#89) were perverting the ways of the Lord, he took a strong group of missionaries with him to Antionum to preach to the people. Omner was among those who went with Alma[2]. The missionaries went their separate ways to preach. The Lord provided for their needs in answer to Alma's[2] prayer of faith.

Alma 35. After preaching among the Zoramites[2], the missionaries [including Omner] returned to Jershon. When the people of **Ammon**[2] or **Ammonites** (#84) left Jershon and went to Melek so the Nephite armies could use Jershon as a base camp, Omner, Alma[2] and their brethren returned to Zarahemla.

54. HIMNI

Mosiah 27:8, 34. **HIMNI** was one of the four sons of **Mosiah**[2] (*#32*) who first persecuted the church. After an angel appeared unto him, his brothers and **Alma**[2] (*#50*), he spent the rest of his life as a missionary.

Mosiah 28. He, like his brothers, refused to be king. He spent 14 years, along with his brothers, as a missionary to the **Lamanites** (*#12*) [c. 91-77 B.C.]. At the end of the time with the Lamanites, he and his brothers accidentally met up with Alma[2] as he was traveling to the land of Manti and they were on their way to Zarahemla. They reported on the happenings of the past 14 years.

Alma 17-26. These chapters detail their missionary experiences. For details in this document, see **Aaron's**[3] (*#52*) Missionary Experiences [Alma 21-26]. Himni, **Omner** (*#53*) and Aaron[3] traveled together, but Aaron[3] seems to have been the leader of this group of missionaries.

Alma 31. When Alma[2] received a report that the **Zoramites**[2] (*#89*) were perverting the ways of the Lord, he took a strong group of missionaries with him to Antionum to preach to the people. Himni did not go with them but was left to help in the church in Zarahemla.

8

People First Mentioned in the Book of Alma

55. NEHOR²

Alma 1:2, 15. <u>NEHOR</u>² was a **Nephite** (#13) apostate. [Nehor¹ (SB #4), the brother of **Abraham** (SA #16), is not mentioned in The Book of Mormon.] Nehor² introduced priestcraft among the people and established a false church. He slew **Gideon** (#47) because Gideon contended with him regarding the church. He was condemned to death. He suffered an ignominious death atop the hill Manti after he acknowledged that he had taught the people falsely. This occurred in the first year of the reign of the judges.

56. AMLICI

Alma 2:1. <u>AMLICI</u> was a **Nephite** (#13) dissenter who wanted to be king. The people gathered together and voted against Amlici. He drew many people away who wanted to make him their king. He and his people went to battle against **Alma**² (#50) and the Nephites. As they were retreating, they joined up with the **Lamanites** (#12) and again engaged in battle with Alma² and his people. He was slain in battle by Alma² in the fifth year of the reign of the judges.

Alma 3. Amlici's followers were called **Amlicites** (#57), and they marked themselves by putting a red mark on their foreheads [v. 13]. Thus, they fulfilled the words of God which he said to Nephi¹ (#6): "I will set a mark upon him that mingleth his seed with thy bretheren, that they may be cursed also" [v. 15].

57. AMLICITES

Alma 2:11. <u>AMLICITES</u> were followers of Amlici (#56), an apostate **Nephite** (#13). They wanted a king. They went to battle against **Alma**[2] (#50) and his people. After suffering a loss of 12,532 souls, they joined up with the **Lamanites** (#12). The Nephites lost 6,562 people in the battle.

Alma 3. They marked themselves by putting a red mark on their foreheads after the manner of the Lamanites, although they did not shave their heads like the Lamanites. They came out in open rebellion against God.

58. ZERAM

Alma 2:22. <u>ZERAM</u> was one of four **Nephite** (#13) spies sent by **Alma**[2] (#50) to watch the camp of the **Amlicites** (#57). They reported that **Amlici** (#56) and his people had joined with a large army of **Lamanites** (#12) and were headed for their city.

59. AMNOR

Alma 2:22. <u>AMNOR</u> was one of four **Nephite** (#13) spies sent by **Alma**[2] (#50) to watch the camp of the **Amlicites** (#57). They reported that **Amlici** (#56) and his people had joined with a large army of **Lamanites** (#12) and were headed for their city.

60. MANTI

Alma 2:22. <u>MANTI</u> was one of four **Nephite** (#13) spies sent by **Alma**[2] (#50) to watch the camp of the Amlicites (#57). These spies reported that **Amlici** (#56) and his people had joined up with a large army of **Lamanites** (#12), and they were headed for their city.

61. LIMHER

Alma 2:22. <u>LIMHER</u> was one of four **Nephite** (#12) spies sent by **Alma**[2] (#50) to watch the camp of the **Amlicites** (#57). These spies reported that **Amlici** (#56) and his people had joined up with a large army of **Lamanites** (#12), and they were headed for their city.

62. NEPHIHAH (2)

Alma 4:16-17. **NEPHIHAH** was the second chief judge. He was a wise man who was among the elders of the church and was selected by **Alma**² (#50) and by the voice of the people to be the chief judge so Alma² could devote full time to preaching the gospel. He filled the judgment seat with perfect uprightness before God.

He refused to take possession of the records from Alma² so Alma² passed them on to his son **Helaman**² (#91).

Alma 50. Nephihah died in the 24th year of the reign of the judges, just as peace was restored after **Teancum** (#104) killed **Morianton**² (#103) in battle. After his death, his son **Pahoran**¹ (#105) was appointed to fill the judgment-seat.

63. AMMONIHAHITES

Alma 8:6. The **AMMONIHAHITES** would not hearken to **Alma**² (#50) when he went to preach to them, but cast him out from their midst.

Alma 10. Alma² and **Amulek** predicted the destruction of the Ammonihahites [v.23].

Alma 14. They burned the scriptures and slew the believers. Alma² and Amulek were imprisoned by them. The prison walls fell on the leaders, killing them. Alma² and Amulek were freed, and the people fled from the prophets.

Alma 15. The Ammonihahites were "of the profession of **Nehor**²" (#55), and they cast Alma² and Amulek out when they went to preach to them. They did not believe in repenting of their sins [v. 15].

Alma 16. The **Lamanites** (#12) destroyed the people of Ammonihah. The bodies were piled so deep and the stench was so foul that people did not go in to possess the land of Ammonihah for many years. It was called the Desolation of Nehors.

64. AMULEK

Alma 8:19, 21. <u>AMULEK</u> was the son of **Giddonah**[1] (#65), who was the son of **Ishmael**[2] (#66), who was a descendant of **Aminadi** (#67), who interpreted the writing which was upon the wall of the temple, which was written by the finger of God. Amulek befriended **Alma**[2] (#50) in Ammonihah and gave him food [an angel having shown him Alma[2] in a vision], and then accompanied him to preach the Gospel. They could not be confined in dungeons because the Lord was with them.

Alma 10. It was the fourth day of the seventh month of the tenth year of the reign of the judges when the angel appeared to Amulek. Amulek told the people of Ammonihah that he was very wealthy and had many friends and relatives. He recounted how an angel of the Lord appeared unto him and told him to receive a holy man of God. This holy man was Alma[2]. As Amulek and Alma[2] tried to preach to the people, the lawyers tried to find cause that they might deliver them to their judges to be judged according to the law and then be slain or cast into prison. **Zeezrom** (#68) was the foremost to accuse Amulek and Alma[2] of reviling against their laws.

Alma 11. The Nephite monetary system is set forth. The lawyers tried to keep the people agitated so more lawsuits would be brought to them so they could get more money; therefore, they kept the people riled against Alma[2] and Amulek. Zeezrom tried to bribe Amulek into denying the existence of a Supreme Being. Amulek contended with him. Zeezrom continued questioning Amulek, and Amulek taught that **Christ** (#143) will not save people in their sins. Only those who inherit the kingdom of heaven are saved. All men shall rise in immortality and not even a hair of the head will be lost [v. 44]. There is no death after the resurrection.

Alma 12. Alma[2] contended with Zeezrom, expounding upon things beyond that which Amulek had explained. Zeezrom became convinced of the power of God.

Alma 14. Some people were converted; the majority were not. Alma[2] and Amulek were bound and taken before their chief judge. The people testified against Alma[2] and Amulek. Zeezrom was encircled about by the pains of his own guilt because of the blindness of the minds of the people which he had caused among them by his lying words. He tried to convince the people that he was guilty and that Alma[2] and Amulek were spotless before God. The people then reviled against him, too. The believers and their holy scriptures were burned by fire. The Lord constrained Alma[2] to not interfere. These martyrs would be received by the Lord in glory and their blood would stand as a witness against the people at the last day. Alma[2] and Amulek were cast into prison. They were hit, spit on and mocked. After many days, on the 12th day of the 10th month in the 10th year of the judges, as the chief judge and people were mocking Alma[2] and Amulek, the cords binding Alma[2] and Amulek were broken and the people fell down in fear, unable to flee. An earthquake caused the prison walls to collapse. Everyone within the prison walls except Alma[2] and Amulek was killed.

Alma 15. Alma[2] and Amulek left Ammonihah and traveled to the land of Sidom. The people who had been cast out of Ammonihah because of their faith were gathered there. Zeezrom had also been kicked out but he lay sick with a burning fever in Sidom because of the guilt he felt due to his earlier wickedness. He called for Alma[2] and Amulek to come to him. Alma[2] healed Zeezrom, baptized him, and established the church in Sidom. Meanwhile, Amulek had left all of his riches for the gospel and was rejected by his friends, his father, and his kindred. Therefore, Alma[2] took Amulek back to Zarahemla with him to his own house, administered unto him in his tribulations, and strengthened him in the Lord.

Alma 31. Amulek went with Alma[2] and a group of missionaries to preach to the **Zoramites**[2] (#89). They found strange forms of worship: the poor were being denied access to the synagogues by the wealthier Zoramites[2].

Alma 34. Amulek testified that the word is in Christ unto salvation. He preached that unless an atonement is made, all mankind must perish. The whole law of Moses points toward the sacrifice of the Son of God. If we do all things but turn away the sick and the needy, our prayers availeth us nothing. He also taught that this life is the time for men to prepare to meet God. "I beseech of you that ye do not procrastinate the day of your repentance until the end; for after this day of life, which is given us to prepare for eternity, behold, if we do not improve our time while in this life, then cometh the night of darkness wherein there can be no labor performed" [v. 33].

65. GIDDONAH[1]

Alma 10:2. **GIDDONAH[1]**, the son of **Ishmael[2]** (#66) and the father of **Amulek** (#64), was a descendant of **Aminadi** (#67) who was a descendant of **Nephi[1]** (#6). [**Giddonah[2]** (#87) was a high priest in Gideon.]

Alma 15. Giddonah[1] rejected Amulek when Amulek became converted to the church [v. 16].

66. ISHMAEL[2]

Alma 10:2. **ISHMAEL[2]** was the grandfather of **Amulek** (#64) and the father of Giddonah[1] (#65). King **Lamoni** (#74) was a descendant of Ishmael[2] [Alma 17:21]. [**Ishmael[1]** (#9) and his family left Jerusalem with **Lehi's[1]** (#1) family, 600 B.C. There is another **Ishmael** in the Bible. He was the son of **Abraham** (SA #16) by Hagar, **Sarah's** (SA #17) handmaiden. However, he is not listed in the Index to The Book of Mormon and, therefore, does not have a superscript number affixed to his name. Technically, he should be Ishmael[1].]

67. AMINADI

Alma 10:2. **AMINADI** was a descendant of **Nephi[1]** (#6). We are told that Aminadi "was that same Aminadi who interpreted the writing which was upon the wall of the temple, which was written by the finger of God." Although the Nephites (#13) were apparently familiar with who Aminadi was and the account of his interpreting those writings, we are not provided any further details or background regarding him except that his posterity included **Ishmael[2]** (#66), **Giddonah[1]** (#65) and **Amulek** (#64).

68. ZEEZROM

Alma 10:31. <u>ZEEZROM</u> was a lawyer in Ammonihah [c. 82 B.C.]. He accused **Alma**[2] (#50) and **Amulek** (#64) of preaching and reviling against their laws.

Alma 11. The Nephite monetary system is set forth. The lawyers tried to keep the people agitated so more lawsuits would be brought to them so they could get more money. Therefore, they kept the people riled against Alma[2] and Amulek. Zeezrom tried to bribe Amulek into denying the existence of a Supreme Being. He was caught in his lying. Zeezrom continued questioning Amulek. Amulek taught that **Christ** (#143) will not save people in their sins, only those who inherit the kingdom of heaven are saved, but all men shall rise in immortality. Not even a hair of the head will be lost [v. 44]. There is no death after the resurrection. Zeezrom began to tremble at Amulek's words.

Alma 12. Alma[2] contended with Zeezrom. Zeezrom became convinced of the power of God and inquired diligently of Alma[2] and Amulek to learn concerning the kingdom of God. Alma[2] explained things beyond that which Amulek had explained: the mysteries of God can be given only to the faithful; men will be judged by their thoughts, beliefs, words, and works. He also discussed the plan of redemption and that this life is a probationary and preparatory state.

Alma 14. Zeezrom was astonished at the words which he heard and became "harrowed up under a consciousness of his own guilt" [v. 6] because of the blindness he had caused in the minds of the people by his earlier lying words. He tried to convince the people that Alma[2] and Amulek were right and that he had been wrong, but the people rejected him and cast him out. He went to Sidom.

Alma 15. After being cast out of Ammonihah, Alma[2] and Amulek found Zeezrom sick in Sidon. He had a burning fever related to the great mental distress he experienced due to his earlier wickedness. He feared that Alma[2] and Amulek had been slain and he blamed himself. Alma[2] inquired as to his testimony. After being assured that Zeezrom did believe in the redemption of Christ, Alma[2] prayed in his behalf and

Zeezrom was healed. Alma² then baptized him. Zeezrom began to preach from that time forth.

Alma 31. When Alma² headed up a mission to reclaim the apostate Zoramites² (#89), Zeezrom was among those who went with him [v. 32].

Helaman 5. Later on, when **Aminadab** (#130) was preaching to the **Lamanites** (#12), he reminded them that they had been taught by Alma², Amulek and Zeezrom.

69. ANTIONAH

Alma 12:20. **ANTIONAH** was a chief ruler in Ammonihah when **Alma²** (#50) and **Amulek** (#64) went there to preach. He questioned Alma² about the resurrection and certain scriptures pertaining to the garden of Eden and cherubim and the flaming sword.

70. CHIEF JUDGE OF AMMONIHAH

Alma 14:4. The **CHIEF JUDGE OF AMMONIAH** and his people smote **Alma²** (#50) and **Amulek** (#64) when they were bound. He burned their followers and their records. He taunted Alma² and Amulek. The prison walls fell on him and his followers, killing him and the lawyers, priests and teachers who smote upon Alma² and Amulek, while Alma² and Amulek walked out uninjured.

71. ZORAM²

Alma 16:5. **ZORAM²** was appointed chief captain over the **Nephites** (#13) in 81 B.C., the 11th year of the reign of the judges. [**Zoram¹** (#8) was the servant of **Laban** (#7); **Zoram³** (#90) was a Nephite apostate.] Zoram² had two sons: **Lehi²** (#72) and **Aha** (#73). He and his sons went to **Alma²** (#50) to seek guidance as to where to search in the wilderness for their brethren who had been captured by the **Lamanites** (#12). Zoram² led the Nephites to victory over the Lamanites and rescued all of their people who had been captured.

72. LEHI²

Alma 16:5. <u>**LEHI**</u>² is one of the sons of **Zoram**² (#71). [**Lehi**¹ (#1) led his family out of Jerusalem; **Lehi**³ (#98) was a **Nephite** (#13) military commander and, according to the Index to The Book of Mormon, may be the same person as Lehi²; **Lehi**⁴ (#128) was a great missionary son of **Helaman**² (#91).] Lehi² went with his father and brother to seek **Alma's**² (#50) advice so as to free their people who had been captured by the **Lamanites** (#12).

73. AHA

Alma 16:5. <u>**AHA**</u> was one of the sons of **Zoram**² (#71). He and his brother went with their father to seek **Alma's**² (#50) advice so as to free their people who had been captured by the **Lamanites** (#12).

74. LAMONI

Alma 17:21. <u>**LAMONI**</u> was a **Lamanite** (#12) king. He was a descendant of **Ishmael**² (#66). He offered his daughter in marriage to Ammon² (#51). **Ammon**² declined but offered to be his servant.

Alma 18. When Lamoni heard how Ammon² had fended off marauders who delighted in scattering his flocks, he thought Ammon² must be the Great Spirit. Ammon² said he was not the Great Spirit; he was just a man. When Ammon² asked if Lamoni would believe him if he told him by what power he was able to do the things he did, Lamoni said he would believe. Ammon² taught him and his servants many things, including the fact that in the beginning man was created after the image of God. Lamoni fell to the earth as though dead. He was carried to his bed, and he lay there for two days. His wife and children mourned over him.

Alma 19. **Lamoni's wife** (#75) called Ammon² in to see her husband. Some people thought he "stinketh" and should be placed in a sepulchre, but she didn't think so. Ammon² said Lamoni would rise on the morrow, that he was not dead. Lamoni received the light of everlasting life and saw the **Redeemer** (#143). After Lamoni rose as Ammon² said he would, he, his wife, Ammon², and Lamoni's servants all fell to the earth.

One Lamanite woman, **Abish** (#76), who had been converted years earlier, quickly called the people so they could see what had occurred. However, when the people saw the king, queen, servants and Ammon² fallen, they were divided: some murmured, some were angry. There was great contention. One man, whose brother had been slain by Ammon² at the waters of Sebus, tried to kill Ammon² but fell dead. Others believed Ammon² had been sent by the Great Spirit. Abish reached out and took the queen's hand. She awoke and took Lamoni's hand. They rejoiced in the Lord. When Ammon² awoke, he also rejoiced, and they all preached to the people. Many were converted and baptized.

Alma 20. After establishing the Church there, Ammon² left to go to Middoni. Lamoni went to Middoni with him in order to free Ammon's² brother and brethren from prison because he and the king of Middoni were friends. On the way to Middoni, they met **Lamoni's father** (#80) who was king over all the land. Lamoni's father ordered him to kill Ammon². Lamoni refused, so his father reached out to slay his son. Ammon² stopped him and made him agree to allow Lamoni to retain his kingdom, be free to reign independent of his father, and that he [Lamoni's father] not be angry with Lamoni. Lamoni and Ammon² then continued on to Middoni where they delivered **Aaron**³ (#52), **Muloki** (#77) and **Ammah** (#78) from prison.

Alma 21. Lamoni and Ammon² returned from Middoni to the land of Ishmael. King Lamoni would not have Ammon² serve him or be his servant, but he caused that there should be synagogues built in the land of Ishmael. Lamoni preached to his people. He also told them they were now a free people and they could worship according to their desires. He then had Ammon² preach to the people.

Alma 24. When Ammon² and his companions saw the preparations the Lamanites were making to destroy the **Anti-Nephi-Lehies** (#84), they traveled to the land of Ishmael in order to hold a council with Lamoni and his brother, king **Anti-Nephi-Lehi** (#85), to discuss what they should do to defend themselves against the Lamanites. However, having been converted, and fearing that if they should resort to the sword again they might not be forgiven again, they decided to bury their weapons of war and suffer death, if necessary, at the hands of the Lamanites rather

than defend themselves. One thousand and five were killed as they prostrated themselves on the ground. Seeing their willingness to die rather
than fight, more Lamanites were converted than had been slain.

Alma 27. The **Amalekites** (#81) again stirred the Lamanites to anger
against their brethren, the people of Anti-Nephi-Lehi, and began to
destroy them. The Anti-Nephi-Lehies again refused to take up arms to
defend themselves. When Ammon[2] and his brethren saw this great work
of destruction among these people whom they loved, they suggested,
"Let us gather this people of the Lord, and let us go down to the land of
Zarahemla to our brethren the **Nephites** (#13), and flee out of the hands
of our enemies, that we be not destroyed" [v. 5].

75. LAMONI'S WIFE

Alma 18:43. <u>**KING LAMONI'S WIFE**</u> and sons and daughters
mourned over his body for two days and two nights when **Lamoni** (#74)
fell to the floor as if dead and his servants carried him to her.

Alma 19. When **Ammon**[2] (#51) told the queen that Lamoni was not dead
and to not bury him, Lamoni's wife believed Ammon[2]. He told her, "I say
unto thee, woman, there has not been such great faith among all the people of the **Nephites**" (#13) [v. 10]. When the king fell into a second trance,
she also fell into a trance along with him, Ammon[2] and Lamoni's servants.
Abish (#76) summoned the people. When the people saw their king and
queen fallen, contention broke out. Abish touched the queen's hand and the
queen arose. Lamoni's wife then caused Lamoni to arise. Ammon[2] and the
servants arose. They were all converted and taught the people.

76. ABISH

Alma 19:16. <u>**ABISH**</u> was a **Lamanite** (#12) woman, a servant of
Lamoni (#74), who had been converted many years earlier because of a
remarkable vision of her father, but she had not let it be known. She
spread the word that the king, queen, Ammon[2] and the servants had all
fallen into a trance, but was distressed to return to find all the people who
had come to witness the scene in contention one with another. She took
the queen's hand and awakened her from her trance.

77. MULOKI

Alma 20:2. <u>MULOKI</u> was a missionary companion to **Aaron**[3] (#52). He was imprisoned with him in Middoni.

Alma 21. Muloki preached in Ani-Anti along with **Ammah** (#78). They went with Aaron[3] to Middoni to preach and were imprisoned there. They were freed by **Ammon**[2] (#51) and **Lamoni** (#74).

78. AMMAH

Alma 20:2. <u>AMMAH</u> was a missionary companion to **Aaron**[3] (#52). He was imprisoned with him in Middoni.

Alma 21. He, along with **Muloki** (#77), was preaching in Ani-Anti when Aaron[3] arrived there. They were not meeting with much success so they accompanied Aaron[3] to Middoni to preach and were imprisoned there. They were freed by **Ammon**[2] (#51) and **Lamoni** (#74).

79. ANTIOMNO

Alma 20:4. <u>ANTIOMNO</u> was the king over Middoni and had imprisoned **Aaron**[3] (#52), **Muloki** (#77) and **Ammah** (#78). He was a friend of king **Lamoni** (#74). King Lamoni accompanied **Ammon**[2] (#51) to Middoni and used his influence with Antiomno to have these three missionaries released from prison.

80. LAMONI'S FATHER

Alma 20:8. <u>LAMONI'S FATHER</u> was king over all the land. He ordered **Lamoni** (#74) to kill **Ammon**[2] (#51). When Lamoni refused to do so, he tried to slay Lamoni. Ammon[2] stopped him. Then Lamoni's father tried to slay Ammon[2], but Ammon[2] withstood his blows and smote his arm so that he could not use it. Ammon[2] granted Lamoni's father his life. In return, Lamoni's father agreed to Ammon's[2] demands that Lamoni be allowed to retain his kingdom, be free to reign independent of his father, and that he [Lamoni's father] not be angry with Lamoni.

Alma 22. After **Aaron**[3] (#52) and his brethren were freed from prison in Middoni by Ammon[2] and king Lamoni, they went to the land of Nephi to the house of Lamoni's father. They offered to be his servants, which he declined, but he wanted them to explain some things to him. He indicated that he had been somewhat troubled in mind because of Ammon's[2] generosity and kindness to him. They taught him about the Spirit of the Lord, or the Great Spirit, as he referred to him. Aaron[3] explained all the scriptures to him, beginning from the creation of Adam. He was taught about the plan of redemption and **Christ's** (#143) atonement. Lamoni's father inquired as to what he had to do to gain eternal life and indicated he would give away all his sins to know God. He was struck as though dead.

The servants ran to the **queen** (#83), who ordered Aaron[3] and his brethren to be slain. The servants had witnessed what had happened and refused. The queen sent for others to do it. Aaron[3] put forth his hand and raised the king. Lamoni's father, the queen and their whole household were converted. The king spoke to the people and administered unto them. He caused that Aaron[3] and his brethren should preach to the people.

Alma 23. The king sent a proclamation throughout all the land that the people should not lay their hands on Ammon[2], Aaron[3], **Omner** (#53) and **Himni** (#54), nor on any of their brethren, but the people should allow them to have free access to their houses, their temples and their sanctuaries to preach to them. Thousands were converted. The king and those who were converted desired to have a name that they could take upon themselves to distinguish them from the non-believers. The name they decided upon was **Anti-Nephi-Lehies** (#84).

Alma 24. The king named one of his sons **Anti-Nephi-Lehi** (#85) and conferred the kingdom upon him. The king died that same year.

81. AMALEKITES

Alma 21:2. The <u>**AMALEKITES**</u> were a group of apostate **Nephites** (#13) [c. 90 B.C.]. Together with the **Amulonites** (#82), they built a great city called Jerusalem. The Amalekites and Amulonites were even more hardened than the **Lamanites** (#12). They built synagogues after the order of **Nehor**[2] (#55); and they mocked **Aaron**[3] (#52) when he preached among them, so he left and went to Ani-Anti and then to Middoni.

Alma 22. King **Lamoni's father** (#80) said the Amalekites believed in a God [v. 7].

Alma 23. The Amalekites were so hardened that only one Amalekite was ever converted to the true church established by **Alma**[2] (#50).

Alma 24. The Amalekites and the Amulonites continued to stir up their people and the non-converted Lamanites against their brethren, the **Anti-Nephi-Lehies** (#84).

Alma 43. Because the Amalekites were of a more wicked and murder-ous disposition than the Lamanites, they were appointed chief captains over the Lamanites by **Zerahemnah** (#96). When they came against the Nephites in battle, the Lamanites were not protected with breastplates nor shields as the Nephites were, so they were afraid of them and didn't come against the Nephites in the borders of Jershon, but they hoped to attack a less fortified group in the land of Manti. The Lord, through Alma[2], told **Moroni**[1] (#97) where the Lamanites were headed. As a result, they fortified and defended the land of Manti.

Alma 44. Moroni[1] demanded that Zerahemnah surrender. Zerahemnah was willing to surrender his weapons up unto Moroni[1], but he refused to promise not to come against them in battle again. Thus, Moroni[1] said they'd finish the battle right then. Zerahemnah rushed at Moroni[1] to kill him, but one of Moroni's[1] soldiers [Lehi[3] (#98)] scalped Zerahemnah and the battle continued. The Lamanites [including the Amalekites and Amulonites] under Zerahemnah, were ultimately defeated; Zerahemnah promised that if Moroni[1] would spare the lives of those who remained, they would covenant to never come against them in battle again.

82. AMULONITES

Alma 21:3. The **AMULONITES** were the descendants and followers of **Amulon** (#48) and the **priests of Noah**[3] (#43). They and the **Amalekites** (#81) had built a great city which they called Jerusalem. They were more

hardened and more wicked than the **Lamanites** (#12) and were after the
order of **Nehor**[2] (#55).

Alma 23. Even when thousands of Lamanites were converted, not one
of the Amulonites was converted.

Alma 24. They rebelled against the king, **Lamoni's father** (#80), and
went to war against the people of **Anti-Nephi-Lehi** (#85). They killed
those who believed in **Christ** (#143).

Alma 25. When the **Anti-Nephi-Lehies** (#84) preferred to suffer death
rather than take up the sword, the Amulonites, which included the priests
of Noah[3], were angrier than ever with the **Nephites** (#13) and had many
battles with them. Among those Lamanites who were killed in battle
were almost all the seed of Amulon and the priests of Noah[3]. Those who
escaped usurped power and authority over the Lamanites. The
Lamanites eventually became angry with those who had usurped power
over them so they hunted the seed of Amulon and killed them. Thus,
Abinadi's (#44) prophecy was fulfilled.

83. LAMONI'S MOTHER

Alma 22:19. **LAMONI'S MOTHER** is not mentioned by name but is
simply referred to as the queen. [She was probably Lamoni's mother.]
When the **king** (#80) was struck as if dead while **Aaron**[3] (#52) was
preaching to him, the servants ran to tell the queen. She ordered the servants to slay Aaron[3] and his brethren. They dared not, so she told them
to call the people to come and slay Aaron[3] and his brothers. However,
Aaron[3] put forth his hand and raised the king. The king immediately
started ministering to his people. His whole household, including the
queen, were converted.

84. ANTI-NEPHI-LEHIES

Alma 23:17. **ANTI-NEPHI-LEHIES** [also called **AMMONITES** and
THE PEOPLE OF AMMON[2]] were converted **Lamanites** (#12).
When **Aaron**[3] (#52) and his brethren preached to **Lamoni's father**
(#80) and his people, many thousands of Lamanites were converted and
they joined those who had been converted by **Ammon**[2] (#51). They

chose to call themselves Anti-Nephi-Lehies so as to distinguish themselves from those who were not converted. As many as were converted never fell away. Later on, they were called Ammonites. They became a very industrious people, very friendly with the **Nephites** (#13), and the curse of God no longer followed them.

Alma 24. They buried their weapons of war and determined that they would rather die than kill again. Thus, when their unconverted brethren came against them in battle, they prostrated themselves on the ground. One thousand and five were slain, but when the Lamanites saw that they would not fight, more Lamanites were converted than had been killed. The ones who did the killing were mostly the **Amalekites** (#81) and the **Amulonites** (#82) rather than the descendants of **Laman**[1] (#3) and **Lemuel** (#4). It was these Lamanites who were converted. [No Amulonite and only one Amalekite was converted .]

Alma 25. When the Lamanites saw that they could not defeat the Nephites, they dispersed. Many came over to the land of Nephi and joined the Anti-Nephi-Lehies. They also buried their weapons of war. They observed the law of Moses and looked forward to the coming of **Christ** (#143).

Alma 27. When the Amalekites saw that they could not defeat the Nephites, they took revenge on their brethren, the Anti-Nephi-Lehies. Again, these people would not take up arms to defend themselves but would suffer death instead. When Ammon[2] and his brethren saw this terrible destruction, they suggested to the king that they flee from their enemies and all go down to the land of Zarahemla. The king was concerned that the Nephites would destroy them because of all the murders they had previously committed. However, after Ammon[2] inquired of the Lord whether or not they should go, they agreed to go with him. When they neared Zarahemla, Ammon[2] and his brethren had the Anti-Nephi-Lehies wait while they went ahead to inquire of the chief judge concerning admitting these people to their land. On the way there, Ammon[2] and his brethren ran into **Alma**[2] (#50) after having not seen him for 14 years. Alma[2] conducted his brethren back to Zarahemla. The chief judge and all the people said they would welcome the Anti-Nephi-Lehies and would give them the land of Jershon, where they could protect them, for a land of inheritance. After they were settled in the land of Jershon, the Anti-Nephi-Lehies were called the people of Ammon[2] and were distinguished by that name from then on.

Alma 35. The **Zoramites**[2] (#89) were furious with the Ammonites for welcoming all those whom the Zoramites[2] cast out. Therefore, they stirred up the Lamanites against the people of Ammon[2] and made preparations for war. The Ammonites left Jershon and went into Melek so the Nephite armies could use Jershon as a base of operation. War commenced in the 18th year of the judges.

Alma 43. Because the people of Ammon[2] had vowed to never take up arms again, the Nephites had to do battle without them. However, the people of Ammon[2] gave a large portion of their substance to support the Nephite armies who were led by **Moroni**[1] (#97).

Alma 47. When **Amalickiah** (#99) had king **Lehonti** (#102) killed, the king's servants fled and joined the people of Ammon[2].

Alma 53. Wars had been raging for approximately nine years [73 B.C. to 64 B.C.], and the people of Ammon[2] were moved with compassion for the Nephites who defended them. As a result, they considered taking up arms in defense of their country. However, **Helaman**[2] (#91) and his brethren persuaded them to refrain from doing that for fear that if they broke their oath, they would lose their souls. However, the Ammonites had 2000 sons who had not taken the oath to never take up arms, and they assembled themselves together and asked Helaman[2] to be their leader.

Alma 56. These sons were very valiant, and they defeated the Lamanites. Not one of these 2000 young men was slain.

Alma 62. In the commencement of the 31st year of the reign of the judges, war continued. Moroni[1] and **Pahoran**[1] (#105) encountered a large group of Lamanites. They killed many of them and captured 4,000 which they sent to dwell with the people of Ammon[2], causing them to covenant that they would not take up their weapons of war against the Nephites again.

Helaman 3. By the 43rd year of the reign of the judges [46 B.C.], there was no contention among the Nephites. However, by the 46th year there was much contention and many people departed out of the land of Zarahemla into the land northward. Many of the people of Ammon² also went into this northern land.

85. ANTI-NEPHI-LEHI

Alma 24:3. <u>ANTI-NEPHI-LEHI</u> was king **Lamoni's** (#74) brother and son of the **king** (#80) who was king over all the land. His father, shortly before his death, conferred the kingdom on Anti-Nephi-Lehi. Anti-Nephi-Lehi held a council with Lamoni, **Ammon²** (#51) and Ammon's² brethren to determine what they should do to defend themselves against the **Lamanites** (#12) who were preparing for battle against them. King Anti-Nephi-Lehi suggested, and it was agreed upon, that if their enemy should come to battle against them, they would hide away their swords. They would bury them in the earth "that they may be kept bright, as a testimony that we have never used them, at the last day; and if our brethren destroy us, behold, we shall go to our God and shall be saved" [v. 16]. They dared not stain their swords with blood again for fear the Lord would not forgive them another time.

86. KORIHOR

Alma 30:6, 12. <u>KORIHOR</u> was Anti-Christ. During the 16th year and the first part of the 17th year of the reign of the judges, there was peace throughout Zarahemla. In the latter part of the 17th year, Korihor came amongst the people, preaching against the prophecies concerning the coming of **Christ** (#143) and his atonement. He led many people away. Korihor then went to Jershon, but the **people of Ammon²** (#84) bound him up and carried him before **Ammon²** (#51), who was their high priest [v. 20]. Ammon² had him carried out of the land.

Korihor then went to the land of Gideon and was taken before the chief judge and also before the high priest **Giddonah²** (#87). Giddonah² and the chief judge ordered him to be bound and taken to Zarahemla to be brought before **Alma²** (#50) and the **chief judge** (#88) who was governor over all the land. Korihor contended with Alma[2] and implied that Alma[2] wanted the people to join the church just so Alma[2] could get gain. Alma[2] reminded him that he did not get paid for preaching, and he provided for his own needs by working. Korihor demanded a sign and was finally given one: he was struck dumb. He then wrote that Satan appeared to him as an angel and told him to reclaim the people. He asked for the curse to be taken from him. Alma[2] refused because Korihor would only lead the people astray again. He was cast out and wandered from house to house, begging for food for his support. His wanderings took him to the land of the **Zoramites**[2] (#89). As he went forth among them, he was run upon and trodden to death.

87. GIDDONAH[2]

Alma 30:23. <u>GIDDONAH</u>[2] was a high priest in Gideon. He was challenged by **Korihor** (#86) who was Anti-Christ. When Giddonah[2] and the chief judge saw the futility of reasoning with Korihor, they had him bound and delivered to **Alma**[2] (#50) and the **chief judge in Zarahemla** (#88). [**Giddonah**[1] (#65) was **Amulek's** (#64) father.]

88. CHIEF JUDGE IN ZARAHEMLA

Alma 30:29. The <u>CHIEF JUDGE IN ZARAHEMLA</u> was governor over all the land. When **Korihor** (#86) challenged **Alma**[2] (#50) and was struck dumb, the chief judge made this insightful comment to Korihor, "Art thou convinced of the power of God? In whom did ye desire that Alma[2] should show forth his sign? Would ye that he should afflict others, to show unto thee a sign? Behold, he has showed unto you a sign; and now will ye dispute more?" [v. 51].

89. ZORAMITES[2]

Alma 30:59. These <u>ZORAMITES</u>[2] were apostate **Nephites** (#13). They were led by **Zoram**[3] (#90). [The earlier **Zoramites**[1] (#16), descendants of **Zoram**[1] (#8), were true believers in **Christ** (#143).]

Alma 31. **Alma**[2] (#50) and his brethren went to preach to them. They discovered a strange form of worship. "They had a place built up in the center of their synagogue, a place for standing, which was high above the head; and the top thereof would only admit one person. Therefore, whosoever desired to worship must go forth and stand upon the top thereof, and stretch forth his hands towards heaven, and cry with a loud voice, saying, 'Holy, holy God; we believe that thou are God, and we believe that thou art holy, and that thou wast a spirit, and that thou art a spirit, and that thou wilt be a spirit forever. Holy God, we believe that thou hast separated us from our brethren; and we do not believe in the tradition of our brethren, which was handed down to them by the child-ishness of their fathers; but we believe that thou hast elected us to be thy holy children; and also thou hast made it known unto us that there shall be no Christ . . . And again we thank thee, O God, that we are a chosen and a holy people. Amen'" [vs. 15-18]. Every man gave the same prayer. The place was called Rameumptom, which means, the holy stand. After praying they returned to their homes, never speaking of God again until they had assembled themselves together again to the holy stand to offer up thanks after this same manner.

Alma 32. The poor were not allowed to pray in the synagogues. Alma[2] taught them that they didn't have to worship only in synagogues. He compared the word unto a seed.

Alma 35. The preaching of the word destroyed the craft of the Zoramites[2]. They expelled the converts, who then joined **the people of Ammon**[2] (**Anti-Nephi-Lehies,** #84) in Jershon. Alma[2] sorrowed because of the wickedness of the people.

Alma 43. In the 18th year of the reign of the judges, the Zoramites[2] became **Lamanites** (#12) and came to battle against the Nephites. Their leader was **Zerahemnah** (#96). Zerahemnah appointed chief captains from among the **Amalekites** (#81) and Zoramites[2] because they were of a more wicked and murderous disposition than were the Lamanites.

90. ZORAM[3]

Alma 30:59. **ZORAM,**[3] an apostate **Nephite** (#12) around 74 B.C., was the leader of a group of apostate Nephites called **Zoramites**[2] (#89).

[**Zoram**[1] (#8) was a servant of **Laban** (#7). **Zoram**[2] (#71) was a Nephite chief captain.]

Alma 31. **Alma**[2] (#50) journeyed to the Zoramites[2] because he got word that they were perverting the ways of the Lord and that Zoram[3] was leading them to bow down to dumb idols. The Zoramites[2] had gathered themselves together in a land called Antionum, east of the land of Zarahemla. Alma[2] took several others with him: **Ammon**[2] (#51), **Aaron**[3] (#52), **Omner** (#53), **Amulek** (#64) and **Zeezrom** (#68). Alma[2] also took his sons **Shiblon** (#92) and **Corianton** (#93). His eldest son, Helaman[2] (#91), did not go with them, nor did **Himni** (#54), who was left in the church in Zarahemla.

91.* HELAMAN[2]

Alma 31:7. __HELAMAN__[2] was the eldest son of **Alma**[2] (#50). [**Helaman**[1] (#34) was one of king **Benjamin's** (#30) sons. **Helaman**[3] (#118) was the son of Helaman[2].] His brothers were **Shiblon** (#92) and **Corianton** (#93). Helaman[2] was not taken to preach to the **Zoramites**[2] (#89), but his brothers were.

COMMANDMENTS OF ALMA[2] TO HIS SON HELAMAN[2] (Alma 36-37)

Inasmuch as ye keep the commandments of God, ye shall prosper in the land.

Remember the captivity of our fathers, they were delivered by God.

Whosoever shall put their trust in God shall be supported in their trials and their troubles and their afflictions and shall be lifted up at the last day.

Alma[2] testified to Helaman[2] of his conversion by an angel. He suffered the pains of a damned soul; he called upon the name of **Jesus** (#143), and was then born of God. Sweet joy filled his soul. He saw concourses of angels praising God. His converts have tasted and seen as he did.

Helaman[2] was commanded to take charge of the records which had been entrusted to Alma[2], and to keep a record of his people as Alma[2] had been doing " . . . that by small and simple things are great things brought to pass; and small means in many instances doth confound the wise. And the Lord God doth work by means to bring about his great and eternal purposes; and by very small means the Lord doth confound the wise and bringeth about the salvation of many souls" [Alma 37:6-7]. Alma[2] stressed that it is wisdom in God that these things should be preserved. He told Helaman[2] that if he transgressed the commandments of God, these things which are sacred would be taken away from him by the power of God, and he would be delivered up unto Satan that he may sift him as chaff before the wind. If he kept the commandments of God, no power of earth or hell could take the sacred records from him, for God is powerful to the fulfilling of all his words.

Alma[2] discussed the 24 plates containing the Jaredite record with Helaman[2]. He told him the Lord said that he would prepare unto his servant **Gazelem** (#94) a stone [or interpreters]. Alma[2] explained about the importance of these interpreters.

Helaman[2] was instructed by his father to preach repentance and faith on the Lord Jesus Christ unto the people.

Helaman[2] was instructed regarding the Liahona. Just as the compass pointed the people in the direction they should go, so it is that the word of Christ will point us to a straight course to eternal bliss.

Note: This concludes the commandments of Alma[2] to his son Helaman[2].

Alma 43. Alma[2] and his sons, including Helaman[2], preached the word.

Alma 45. Alma[2] turned the records over to Helaman[2] in the 18th year of the reign of the judges. He then left for Melek and was never heard of again. In the 19th year of the judges, Helaman[2] and his brethren preached the gospel to the people. They built up the church and appointed priests and teachers throughout the land. There arose dissenters.

Alma 46. The leader of the dissenters who opposed Helaman[2] and his brethren and sought to slay them was a large, strong man named **Amalickiah** (*#*99). Amalickiah led many away from the church and hoped they would establish him as king and ruler over them. **Moroni**[1] (*#*97), chief commander of the Nephite armies, rent his coat and wrote upon it and called it the title of liberty. He led the people in preparing themselves to defend themselves against Amalickiah and the **Lamanites** (#12) and **Amalichiahites** (#101), as well as to be faithful to God. Meanwhile, Helaman[2] and his brethren continued to strengthen the Church, whose members were called **Christians** (#100) by those who were not members.

Alma 53. Helaman[2] and his brethren persuaded the **Ammonites** (*#*84) to refrain from breaking the oath that they would never take up weapons again as they considered doing when they saw the suffering of the **Nephites** (#13) in their behalf. However, their sons had never given such an oath, so 2,000 of them entered into a covenant to fight for liberty. They asked Helaman[2] to be their leader.

Alma 56. In the 30th year of the judges, Helaman[2] wrote an epistle to Moroni[1] detailing the events of the past four years: in the 26th year, the 2,000 **sons of the Ammonites** who were also called **sons of Helaman**[2] (#110), asked him to be their leader; they marched to Judea to assist Antipus (#112) and joined with his army. Many cities had been lost to the Lamanites. They engaged in battle with the Lamanites. Antipus had fallen by the sword in battle. Helaman's[2] sons were all spared. Many Lamanite prisoners were taken and they had been sent to Zarahemla.

Alma 57. In the 28th year, Helaman[2] retook the city of Antiparah after the inhabitants fled following **Ammoron's** (#108) refusal to exchange prisoners. In the 29th year, they received provisions and reinforcements including an additional 60 sons of the Ammonites. They captured the city of Cumeni. Their prisoners were so numerous that guarding them became a problem so they decided to send them down to Zarahemla. Those guarding the prisoners, **Gid** (#113) and his soldiers, returned in time to save Helaman[2] and the other warriors from Lamanite defeat. One thousand Nephites had been slain, but none of the sons of Helaman[2] were killed.

Alma 58. Helaman's[2] report continued: In the 29th year, he, Gid and **Teomner** (#114) retook the city of Manti by decoying the Lamanite army out of the city to chase Helaman's[2] warriors while Gid and Teomner captured the city. Helaman[2] and his band headed first in the direction of Zarahemla, but then doubled back to Manti to help maintain the city. Helaman[2] complained somewhat of the lack of government support and wondered why they weren't getting any. They had succeeded in retaking all of their cities in that quarter of the land.

Alma 62. In the 31st year of the reign of the judges, peace was restored among the Nephites. **Pahoran**[1] (#105) returned to the judgment-seat; Moroni[1] turned command of the armies over to **Moronihah**[1] (#116), his son; and Helaman[2] returned to preaching the gospel. Helaman[2] died in the 35th year of the reign of the judges.

92.* SHIBLON

Alma 31:6. <u>SHIBLON,</u> second son of **Alma**[2] (#50), went with his father and his brother **Corianton** (#93), **Ammon**[2] (#51), **Aaron**[3] (#52), **Omner** (#53), **Amulek** (#64) and **Zeezrom** (#68) on a mission to the **Zoramites**[2] (#89).

COMMANDMENTS OF ALMA[2] TO HIS SON SHIBLON (Alma 38)

Alma[2] told him that if he kept the commandments of God, he would prosper in the land. If he didn't, he would be cut off.

He said Shiblon had been a source of great joy and bore persecution and stoning with patience.

Alma[2] told him to trust in God and he would be delivered from trials.

Alma[2] briefly told Shiblon the things he had told **Helaman**[2] (#91) about his conversion.

He stressed that no one can be saved except through **Christ** (#143).

He counseled him to learn wisdom and to continue to teach; to be diligent and temperate in all things; and to bridle passions and refrain from idleness.

Note: This concludes the commandments of Alma² to his son Shiblon.

Alma 43. Alma² and his sons preached the gospel.

Alma 49. Because of the teachings of Shiblon and all the others who had been ordained and sent forth to preach, there was continual peace among the **Nephites** (#13) as the nineteenth year of the judges ended.

Alma 63. In the beginning of the 36th year of the reign of the judges, upon Helaman's² death, Shiblon took possession of the sacred things which had been given to Helaman² by Alma². Prior to Shiblon's death, he passed the sacred records and items on to Helaman's² son **Helaman³** (#118). Shiblon's brother **Corianton** (#93) had gone forth to the land northward in a ship to carry provisions unto the people who had gone forth into that land, so he was not available to care for the records. Shiblon died in the 39th year of the reign of the judges.

93. CORIANTON

Alma 31:6. <u>**CORIANTON,**</u> the older son of **Alma²** (#50), went with his father and his brother **Shiblon** (#92), plus **Ammon²** (#51), **Aaron³** (#52), **Omner** (#53), **Amulek** (#64) and **Zeezrom** (#68) on a mission to the **Zoramites²** (#89).

COMMANDMENTS OF ALMA² TO HIS SON CORIANTON (Alma 39-42)

Alma 39. Alma² chastised Corianton for boasting in his own strength and wisdom and for forsaking the ministry while they were laboring with the Zoramites² and for going into the land of Siron among the borders of the **Lamanites** (#12) after the harlot **Isabel** (#95). Sexual sin is most abominable above all sins except the shedding of blood and denying the Holy Ghost. The Zoramites² would not accept Alma's² words when they saw Corianton's conduct. Alma^2 commanded Corianton to refrain from his iniquities.

He counseled him to "seek not after riches" [v. 14].

Alma^2 taught Corianton about **Jesus Christ** (#143).

Alma 40. He discussed Christ's resurrection and the redemption of the dead. Time is measured only unto men, not unto God. There is a time between death and the resurrection: paradise or a state of misery. After the resurrection comes the judgment. All things shall be restored to their proper and perfect frame; "even a hair of the head shall not be lost" [v. 23]. The state of the wicked will be awful.

Alma 41. All things will be restored to their proper order: good to good, wickedness to wickedness. In the resurrection, men come forth to a state of endless happiness or endless misery. Wickedness never was happiness. The word restoration more fully condemns the sinner, and does not justify him at all.

Alma 42. Alma^2 taught Corianton about **Adam** (SA #4) and **Eve** (SA #5), the garden of Eden and the fall. He also taught him about the atonement of Christ. He instructed him regarding the relationship between sin, repentance, law, punishment, justice and mercy. Mercy cannot rob justice.

Corianton was again called to preach the word unto the people.

Note: This concludes Alma's^2 counsel to his son Corianton.

Alma 43. Alma^2 and his sons preached the gospel.

Alma 63. After Helaman^2 kept the records, they were passed on to Shiblon, who only had then for about three years. Prior to Shiblon's death in the 39th year of the judges, he conferred the records on Helaman's^2 son **Helaman^3** (#118) because Corianton had gone to the land northward in a ship to carry provisions unto the people who had gone forth into that land and was not available to keep the records.

94. GAZELEM

Alma 37:23. <u>GAZELEM</u> is a name given to a servant of God. The Lord said, "I will prepare unto my servant Gazelem, a stone . . . ." These interpreters were prepared that the word of God might be fulfilled.

95. ISABEL

Alma 39:3. <u>ISABEL</u> was a harlot in the land of Siron who stole away the hearts of many and was visited by **Alma's** (#50) son **Corianton** (#93).

96. ZERAHEMNAH

Alma 43:5. <u>ZERAHEMNAH</u> was a **Lamanite** (#12) leader in the war against the **Nephites** (#13) during the 18th year of the reign of judges. He appointed **Amalekites** (#81) and **Zoramites** (#89) who had become Lamanites to be chief captains over the Lamanites because they had a more wicked and murderous disposition. When his armies came against **Moroni's** (#97) armies at Jershon, they were afraid because they were almost naked and Moroni's armies were well protected with breastplates and heavy clothing. When they departed, they intended to secretly come into the land of Manti and take possession of it, but Moroni sent spies to watch their camp.

Alma 44. Moroni's soldiers captured Zerahemnah's soldiers by using stratagem. Through **Alma** (#50), the Lord told Moroni just where to go to look for Zerahemnah's soldiers. Moroni ordered Zerahemnah to surrender. He refused and rushed at Moroni. One of Moroni's soldiers, Lehi (#98), took Zerahemnah's scalp off. Many of Zerahemnah's men then covenanted to make peace and were allowed to depart into the wilderness. The battle resumed. As the Lamanites were about to go down in defeat, Zerahemnah begged for mercy and promised that he and his people would enter into a covenant of peace if they would spare their lives.

97. MORONI

Alma 43:16. <u>MORONI</u> was a righteous **Nephite** (#13) military commander. [**Moroni** (#162), the son of **Mormon** (#159), was the last

Nephite survivor.] At age 25, in the 18th year of the judges, Moroni[1] was appointed chief captain over the Nephites and was in command of all the armies of the Nephites. He prepared his people with breastplates, arm-shields, and also shields to defend their heads. They were also dressed with thick clothing. **Zerahemnah's** (#96) armies had never seen any such thing. The **Lamanite** (#12) armies left and intended to secretly come into the land of Manti to take possession of it, but Moroni[1] sent spies to watch their camp and also sent certain men unto **Alma**[2] (#50) to inquire of the Lord where the Nephite armies should go to defend themselves against the Lamanites. The Lord revealed to Alma[2] the Lamanites' strategy. Moroni[1] and **Lehi**[3] (#98) surrounded the Lamanites with their armies. The Nephites were defending their homes, liberties, families, and religion.

Alma 44. Moroni[1] commanded the Lamanites to make a covenant of peace or be destroyed. Zerahemnah rejected the offer and tried to kill Moroni[1]. Therefore, Lehi[3] scalped Zerahemnah. Many of the Lamanite warriors covenanted with Moroni[1] for peace and were allowed to depart into the wilderness. Zerahemnah resumed the battle. As the Lamanites were about to go down in defeat, Zerahemnah begged for mercy and promised that he and his people would enter into a covenant of peace if Moroni[1] would spare their lives. Thus ended the 18th year of the judges.

Alma 46. During the 19th year of the judges, Moroni[1] rent his coat, wrote upon it, "In memory of our God, our religion, and freedom, and our peace, our wives, and our children" [v. 12], and fastened it upon a pole and raised what he called the title of liberty. He gathered together the believers and went against **Amalickiah** (#99) and his followers. Amalickiah fled with a few followers, and Moroni[1] captured the rest. Those who would not covenant to support the cause of freedom were put to death, "and there were but few who denied the covenant of freedom" [v. 35]. They had four years of peace among themselves, although they were compelled to contend with the Lamanites.

Alma 49. Moroni[1] had the people fortify their cities by digging deep ditches around them so the Lamanites could not capture them. The **Amalickiahites** (#101) and Lamanites unsuccessfully tried to capture the cities of Ammonihah and Noah. Amalickiah cursed God and swore to drink the blood of Moroni[1].

Alma 50. In the 20th year of the reign of the judges, Moroni[1] had the people fortify the rest of their cities by digging up heaps of earth round about them. Upon the top of these ridges of earth he caused that there should be timbers built up to the height of a man. Upon the timbers was a frame of strong, high, pickets. He also caused towers to be built that overlooked the pickets, and had places of security built upon the towers so the Lamanites' arrows and stones could not hurt the Nephites. Then the Nephite armies drove out all the Lamanites who were in the east wilderness into their own lands. They built many cities during this time. They multiplied and became exceedingly rich. They had peace for awhile, but in the 24th year a land dispute arose between the people in the land of Lehi and the land of Morianton. **Morianton**[2] (#103) led his followers northward. He was defeated in battle and killed by **Teancum** (#104).

Alma 51. During the 25th year of the judges, a group called **king-men** (#106) arose among the Nephites. They desired to dethrone **Pahoran**[1] (#105) as chief judge because he would not change the law to provide for kings. Moroni[1] petitioned the governor of the land to ask for permission to compel the king-men to defend their country against the Lamanites or be put to death. Four thousand dissenters were put to death and their remaining leaders were imprisoned until such time as it would be possible to hold trials for them. When Amalickiah led the Lamanites against the Nephites to battle, he was killed by Teancum, who crept into his tent at night and put a javelin through his heart.

Alma 52. **Ammoron** (#108) succeeded his brother, Amalickiah, as king of the Lamanites. He led the Lamanites in battle against the Nephites. While Ammoron battled in one area, Moroni[1], Teancum and Lehi[3] [with their armies] defeated **Jacob**[3] (#109), an apostate Nephite of the **Zoramite**[2] (#89) sect, in another area by using stratagem. Teancum decoyed the Lamanite army under Jacob[3] out of Mulek and led them toward Bountiful. At the same time, part of Moroni's[1] army retook Mulek and the rest of his army came upon the rear of Jacob's[3] army. As the Lamanite army pursued Teancum, they had to make a hasty retreat because Lehi[3] and his men came from Bountiful to pursue them. Jacob[3] was caught between Moroni's[1] men to his rear and Lehi's[3] men from the front. Jacob[3] was killed in the ensuing battle, and Moroni[1] was wounded. Many prisoners were taken by the Nephites.

Alma 53. Dissensions among the Nephites gave rise to Lamanite victories. Moroni[1] instructed Teancum to have the prisoners fortify the city Bountiful.

Alma 54. Ammoron wrote to Moroni[1] requesting an exchange of prisoners. They did some negotiating.

Alma 55. Moroni[1] refused to exchange prisoners. The Nephites, with the help of **Laman**[4] (#111), a former Lamanite, got the Lamanite guards drunk and the prisoners were freed without a battle. The Nephites captured the city of Gid without bloodshed.

Alma 56-58. Moroni[1] received an epistle from **Helaman**[2] (#91) detailing the activities of his soldiers, their battles and their successes, during the 26th-29th years.

Alma 59. Those Lamanites who fled from the quarter of the country where Helaman[2] and his warriors were joined forces with the Lamanites in the part of the country where Moroni[1] was. The Lamanites captured the city of Nephihah. Moroni[1] was angry with his government for having not sent sufficient manpower to maintain that city and for what he perceived to be an indifference concerning the freedom of their country.

Alma 60. Moroni[1] wrote an angry letter to the governor, chastising him and calling him to repentance. He told Pahoran[1] he would come against him in battle if he didn't send help.

Alma 61. Pahoran[1] sent Moroni[1] an epistle detailing the bad situation he was facing. Due to insurrection, he and the **freemen** (#107) had to flee to the city of Gideon. Pahoran[1] requested that Moroni[1] come to his aid, leaving Lehi[3] and Teancum in charge in that part of the land.

Alma 62. Moroni[1] complied with Pahoran's[1] request, and then Pahoran[1] and Moroni[1] retook Zarahemla, killing **Pachus** (#115), the leader of the king-men. Thus ended the 30th year. In the 31st year, Moroni[1] had 6,000 men and provisions sent to assist Helaman's[2] armies and another 6,000 men and supplies sent to the armies of Lehi[3] and Teancum. Meanwhile, Moroni[1] and his army, along with Pahoran[1] and his army, captured the city of Nephihah. Moroni[1] had his men enter the west side of the city with strong cords and ladders. Those Lamanite prisoners who covenanted to never take up arms against the Nephites again were sent to dwell with the **Ammonites** (#84). Those who would not covenant for peace were slain.

Moroni[1] and his soldiers pursued the enemy from city to city until they were met by Lehi[3] and Teancum. All the Lamanite armies were gathered together, led by king Ammoron. Teancum sneaked into Ammoron's tent and killed him. However, Teancum was also killed by Ammoron's servants. The Lamanites were driven out of the land. Thus, the 31st year ended. Pahoran[1] returned to his judgment-seat; Moroni[1] turned command of the armies over to his son **Moronihah**[1] (#116); and Helaman[2] returned to preaching the gospel.

Alma 63. Moroni[1] died in the 36th year of the reign of the judges.

98. LEHI[3]

Alma 43:35. **LEHI[3],** according to the Index to The Book of Mormon, may be the same person as Lehi[2] (#72), the son of **Zoram**[2] (#71). [**Lehi**[1] (#1) led his family out of Jerusalem to the Americas; Lehi[4] (#128), son of **Helaman**[2] (#91), was a great missionary.] When we first read of Lehi[2], it is 81 B.C. When we read of Lehi[3], it is 74 B.C., just seven years later. Lehi[3] is a **Nephite** (#13) military commander under **Moroni**[1] (#97). He had his army encircle the **Lamanites** (#12) led by **Zerahemnah** (#96) as the Lamanites were attempting to capture Manti. This was in the 18th year of the judges.

Alma 52. In the 27th year of the judges, Lehi[3] and his army joined forces with Moroni[1] and **Teancum** (#104). Using stratagem, they defeated the Lamanite army led by **Jacob**[3] (#109) by having Teancum decoy them into a trap.

Helaman 1. In the 41st year, the Lamanites, with Coriantumr[3] (#123), a dissenter from among the Nephites as the leader of their armies, came against the Nephites. **Moronihah**[1] (#116) sent Lehi[3] to head Coriantumr[3] and his Lamanite army before they could get to the city of Bountiful.

Moronihah[1] also headed off the Lamanites. Coriantumr[3] was among those killed in battle.

99. AMALICKIAH

Alma 46:3. **AMALICKIAH** was an apostate **Nephite** (#13) who desired to become king. He was the leader of those who rebelled against the church. The rebellious were, for the greatest part, the lower judges of the land, and they were seeking power which Amalickiah promised them. When **Moroni**[1] (#97) headed off Amalickiah and the **Amalickiahites** (#101) in the wilderness, Amalickiah fled with a small number of his men. The rest were captured by Moroni[1].

Alma 47. Amalickiah and those who fled with him went up to the land of Nephi among the **Lamanites** (#12) and stirred them up against the Nephites. Thus, the Lamanites decided to go to battle against the Nephites. The Lamanite king was angry because part of his army was afraid to go against the Nephites. He appointed Amalickiah commander of that part of his army which was obedient to his commands.

Amalickiah tricked **Lehonti** (#102), leader or king over those Lamanites who refused to go to battle against the Nephites, into coming down from Mount Antipas. The plan Amalickiah concocted allowed Lehonti's army to surround Amalickiah's army and take them prisoners. Thus, when Amalickiah's army pleaded with Amalickiah to let them fall in with Lehonti's men, Amalickiah was made second in command after Lehonti. He had one of his servants gradually poison and kill Lehonti. Then he was made leader and chief commander over the entire army. When he returned with these armies to the Lamanite king, the king, supposing him to be returning victorious and having fulfilled his commands, went out to meet him. However, Amalickiah had his servants go forth to meet the king and bow low before him. When the king put forth his hand to raise them, one servant, acting on Amalickiah's orders, stabbed the king and killed him. The king's own servants then fled out of fear lest they also be killed. Amalickiah told the people that it was the king's servants who killed the king and that "whosoever loved the king, let him go forth, and pursue his servants that they may be slain" [v. 27]. The servants fled into the land of Zarahemla and joined the **people of Ammon**[2] (#84).

When the queen learned of her husband's death, she sent for Amalickiah. He brought his murderous servants with him, and they all testified that the king's own servants killed him. Amalickiah took the queen to wife and became king over all the Lamanites.

Alma 48. Amalickiah spent the 19th year of the reign of the judges obtaining power by fraud and deceit. Meanwhile, Moroni[1] was preparing his people to be faithful and to be able to defend themselves by fortifying their cities.

Alma 49. The invading Lamanites were unable to take the fortified cities of Ammonihah and Noah. All their chief captains were killed attempting to capture the city of Noah. Amalickiah cursed God and swore to drink the blood of Moroni[1] [v. 27]. The 19th year ended.

Alma 51. In the 25th year of the judges, Amalickiah led the Lamanites to battle against the Nephites. They took several of the cities Moroni[1] had fortified. However, as Amalickiah slept in his tent one night, Teancum (#104) slipped in and killed him by putting a javelin through his heart.

Alma 52. Amalickiah's brother **Ammoron** (#108) was appointed king by the people.

100. CHRISTIANS

Alma 46:13. <u>**CHRISTIANS**</u> were true believers in **Christ** (#143) long before his birth. The believers were members of the church of God and were called Christians by those who were not members of the church.

101. AMALICKIAHITES

Alma 46:28. <u>**AMALICKIAHITES**</u> were **Nephite** (#13) dissenters who followed **Amalickiah** (#99). For the most part, they were the lower judges who were seeking power. **Moroni**[1] (#97) captured a majority of them and brought them back to the land of Zarahemla. Those who would not enter into a covenant to support the cause of freedom were put to death, " . . . and there were but few who denied the covenant of freedom" [v. 35].

Alma 49. When Amalickiah sent his followers against the Nephites, "the Lamanites, or the Amalickiahites, were exceedingly astonished at their manner of preparation for war" [v. 9] because they had never seen anything like it before. The Amalickiahites were rebuffed in all their attempts to defeat the Nephites. When all their chief captains had been slain, the defeated armies returned to Amalickiah who swore to drink the blood of Moroni[1]. The 19th year of the judges ended.

102. LEHONTI

Alma 47:10. **LEHONTI** was a **Lamanite** (#12) officer and dissenter who would not go to battle against the **Nephites** (#13). He was made king [v. 6] and leader over the dissenting group. He was tricked by **Amalickiah** (#99) and poisoned to death.

103. MORIANTON[2]

Alma 50:28. **MORIANTON**[2] was a leader of the **Nephite** (#13) people in the city of Morianton. [**Morianton**[1] (#210) was a **Jaredite** (#179).] Morianton[2] and his people got into a property dispute with the people in the land of Lehi. When the people of Lehi fled to **Moroni**[1] (#97) for help, Morianton[2] and his followers decided to flee to the land northward. However, a maid servant who Morianton[2] had beaten fled to Moroni[2] and revealed Morianton's[2] plans. Moroni[1] feared the possible consequences of having enemies on the north and south and of losing the people of Bountiful to Morianton[2] so he sent an army, led by **Teancum** (#104), after them. Morianton's[2] people were very stubborn, and a battle ensued during which Teancum slew Morianton[2].

104. TEANCUM

Alma 50:35. **TEANCUM** was a great **Nephite** (#13) military officer. He tried to keep **Morianton**[2] (#103) from occupying the land northward with the help of people in Bountiful. When a battle ensued, he killed Morianton[2]. The rest of the people of Morianton[2] were brought back and, upon their covenanting to keep the peace, were restored to the land of Morianton. Thus ended the 24th year of the reign of the judges.

Alma 51. During the 25th year of the judges, a group called **king-men** (#106) arose and dissented against the loyal **freemen** (#107). **Moroni**[1] (#97) had to quell this disturbance. Meanwhile, this allowed Amalickiah (#99) to lead the **Lamanites** (#12) in capturing several cities Moroni[1] had fortified. Teancum led a Nephite army against Amalichiah. One night as Amalickiah slept, Teancum slipped into his tent and killed him by putting a javelin through his heart.

Alma 52. During the 26th and 27th years of the judges, the Nephites were in dangerous circumstances as the Lamanites made inroads into their territory. In the beginning of the 28th year of the reign of the judges, Moroni[1], Teancum, and many of the chief captains held a council of war to plan strategy on how to get the Lamanites out of their strongholds. **Ammoron** (#108) had been king of the Lamanites now for two years following the death of his brother Amalickiah. Teancum was given orders to make an attack upon the city of Mulek to retake it, if possible. He found it wise to wait for reinforcements from Moroni[1]. Using stratagem, Moroni[1], Teancum and **Lehi**[3] (#98) [who was stationed in Bountiful] and their armies retook Mulek by decoying the Lamanite army out of the city in pursuit of Teancum's army. The Lamanite army, led by **Jacob**[3] (#109), found themselves caught between Moroni's[1] army in their rear and Lehi's[3] army in their front. Jacob[3] was killed and Moroni[1] was wounded. Many Lamanites were taken prisoner.

Alma 62. In the 31st year of the reign of the judges, as the armies of the Nephites united against the united armies of the Lamanites, they met in the land of Moroni. During the night, Teancum crept into king Ammoron's sleeping quarters and killed him. However, he was pursued and killed by Ammoron's servants. Lehi[3] and Moroni[1] were exceedingly sorrowful over his death.

105. PAHORAN[1] (3)

Alma 50:39-40. <u>PAHORAN</u>[1] was the third chief judge. He was appointed at the end of the 24th year of the reign of the judges to fill the judgment-seat when his father, **Nephihah** (#62), died. [**Pahoran**[2] (#119), the son of Pahoran[1], was the fourth **Nephite** (#13) chief judge.]

Alma 60. **Moroni**[1] (#97) wrote an angry letter to Pahoran[1], the governor, chastising him and calling him to repentance. He told him he would come against him in battle if he didn't send help.

Alma 61. Pahoran[1] sent an epistle back to Moroni[1]: the **king-men** (#106) had risen in insurrection and had led many people away. They had come against Pahoran[1] and the **freemen** (#107). Pahoran[1] and his followers had fled from Zarahemla and were in the land of Gideon. He requested that Moroni[1] leave **Lehi**[3] (#98) and **Teancum** (#104) in charge of that part of the land and come to his aid.

Alma 62. Moroni[1] took a small number of his men and went to Pahoran's[1] aid. Moroni[1] and Pahoran[1] and their armies then went to battle against **Pachus** (#115), leader of the king-men in Zarahemla, retaking the city. Pachus was killed and his men taken prisoner. Pahoran[1] was restored to the judgment-seat. Thus ended the 30th year of the judges.

The following year, Pahoran[1] and Moroni[1] retook the city of Nephihah, taking many prisoners. Those who covenanted that they wouldn't go to war against the Nephites again were sent to dwell with the **Ammonites** (#84); those who would not covenant for peace were slain.

Peace was restored among the Nephites. Pahoran[1] returned to the judgment-seat; Moroni[1] yielded up command of the armies to his son **Moronihah**[1] (#116); and **Helaman**[2] (#91) resumed preaching the gospel. [Helaman[2] died four years later; Moroni[1] died five years later.]

Helaman 1. Pahoran[1] died; and in the commencement of the 40th year of the judges, his sons [**Pahoran**[2] (#119), **Paanchi** (#120) and **Pacumeni** (#121)] contended for the judgment-seat.

106. KING-MEN

Alma 51:5. <u>KING-MEN</u> were those people who desired to dethrone **Pahoran**[1] (#105) as chief judge because he would not alter the law to allow for the establishment of a king over the land. These people were of high birth, and they sought to be kings. They were supported by those who wanted power and authority over the people. This all occurred during the

25th year of the judges and was during the same time that **Amalickiah** (#99) was again stirring up the **Lamanites** (#12) to go to battle against the **Nephites** (#13). The king-men would not help defend their country. When the king-men refused to defend their country against the Lamanites, Moroni[1] was given permission to compel them to help defend their country or to put them to death if they refused. Four thousand dissenters were slain, their leaders were temporarily imprisoned, and the rest, rather than be killed, agreed to help defend their country.

Alma 61-62. The king-men rose again in insurrection, forcing Pahoran[1] to flee from Zarahemla to Gideon. Their leader was **Pachus** (#115). Pahoran[1] requested Moroni's[1] help. Together they defeated the king-men, and Pachus was killed. Pachus's men and those king-men who had been imprisoned earlier were tried according to law.

107. FREEMEN

Alma 51:6. FREEMEN were those **Nephites** (#13) who desired that **Pahoran**[1] (#105) should remain chief judge. They swore and covenanted to maintain their rights and the privileges of their religion by a free government. They did not want to change the laws and be ruled by kings.

Alma 61-62. In the 30th year of the judges, when the **king-men** (#106) rose in insurrection, the freemen, along with Pahoran[1], fled to Zarahemla. When **Moroni's**[1] (#97) soldiers came to their aid, the king-men were defeated and the freemen were restored to their lands.

108. AMMORON

Alma 52:3. AMMORON was the brother of **Amalickiah** (#99) and, upon the death of Amalickiah, was appointed to reign as king of the **Lamanites** (#12) in his stead. This was on the first day of the 26th year of the reign of the judges. Ammoron ordered his people to maintain those cities they had captured. Because of the strength of the Lamanites, **Teancum** (#104) decided it was best not to go against Ammoron at this time; he fortified surrounding areas while waiting for reinforcements from **Moroni**[1] (#97).

Teancum was instructed by Moroni[1] to take Lamanite prisoners, when possible, so they could be used as ransom for those **Nephites** (#13) the Lamanites had taken prisoner. While Teancum was busy protecting one quarter of the country, Ammoron slipped away and reported to Amalickiah's wife. He then led a large group to the borders of the west sea which Moroni[1] was defending. Battles continued throughout the 27th and 28th years of the judges.

Alma 54. In the beginning of the 29th year of the judges, Ammoron desired a prisoner exchange. This pleased Moroni[1] exceedingly. Ammoron and Moroni[1] negotiated for the exchange of prisoners. Moroni[1] demanded a man, his wife and his children for one prisoner, and Moroni[1] reminded Ammoron of God's power. Ammoron agreed to the prisoner exchange requirements of Moroni[1] but denied the existence of God and threatened the Nephites with destruction if they didn't subject themselves to the Lamanites.

Alma 55. Moroni[1] refused to exchange prisoners. Instead, he tricked the Lamanite guards into getting drunk, and the Nephite prisoners were freed. The Nephites took the city of Gid without bloodshed.

Alma 56. In the 26th year of the judges, as reported by **Helaman**[2] (#91), Ammoron kept his people from going to war against **Antipus** (#112) and the city of Judea because Helaman[2] had reinforced their armies with his 2,000 warriors.

Alma 57. Helaman[2] also reported that in the 28th year, Ammoron, in an epistle, requested that Helaman[2] deliver up the prisoners he had, and in return he would be given the city of Antiparah. Helaman[2] declined and began war preparations. The people in Antiparah left the city, and it fell into Helaman's[2] hands.

In the 29th year, Helaman[2] and his warriors captured the city Cumeni. However, the number of prisoners they had became burdensome, and they needed to send some to Zarahemla. The men sent to guard the prisoners were led by **Gid** (#113). They met with rebellion from the prisoners when the prisoners overheard some Nephite spies cry out that the armies of the Lamanites were marching toward Cumeni. The majority of the Lamanite prisoners were killed in the rebellion and others escaped. Gid and the rest of the guards quickly returned to Cumeni the following day, just in time to help Helaman² and his warriors who were about to be overpowered because of the additional troops and provisions Ammoron had sent to the Lamanites.

Alma 59. Ammoron continued to strengthen his armies with warriors and supplies; thus, the people of Nephihah were being slaughtered.

Alma 62. The armies of the Lamanites, including Ammoron, were all gathered together by the seashore in battle against the armies of Moroni¹, **Lehi**³ (#98) and Teancum. When they encamped for the night, Teancum climbed over the city wall and located Ammoron sleeping; he blamed him, along with his brother Amalickiah, for the long years of bloodshed. He killed Ammoron by piercing him near the heart with his javelin. Unfortunately, Ammoron cried out, and his servants pursued Teancum and slew him. The 31st year of the reign of the judges ended.

109. JACOB³

Alma 52:20. <u>**JACOB**</u>³ was an apostate **Nephite** (#13) of the **Zoramite**² (#89) sect. [**Jacob**¹ (SA #8) is Israel in the Old Testament; **Jacob**² (#10) is the brother of **Nephi**¹ (#6) and the son of **Lehi**¹ (#1) and **Sariah** (#2).] Jacob³, a leader of the **Lamanite** (#12) army, had an unconquerable spirit. **Teancum** (#104) and a small army, **Moroni**¹ (#97) and his army, and **Lehi**³ (#98) and his army, lured him out of his stronghold. In the ensuing battle, Jacob³ was killed and Moroni¹ was wounded.

110. SONS OF HELAMAN²

Alma 53:16. The "<u>**SONS OF HELAMAN**</u>²" were the sons of the **Ammonites** (#84) who had covenanted that they would never take up arms again. Helaman² (#91) first refers to them as his sons in Alma 56:10. Distressed by the afflictions and tribulations which the **Nephites** (#13) [led by **Moroni**¹ (#97), **Teancum** (#104) and **Lehi**³ (#98) and their armies] suffered in their behalf, these 2,000 sons of the Ammonites [Anti-Nephi-Lehies] having never made an oath to refuse to take up weapons again, covenanted to fight for the liberty of the Nephites and to protect the land unto the laying down of their lives. They asked

Helaman^2 to be their leader. They were exceedingly valiant and walked uprightly before God.

Alma 56. Helaman^2 and his "sons" went to Judea to assist **Antipus** (#112). In the 27th year of the judges, they prepared for war and hoped the **Lamanites** (#12) would come against them. When they didn't, they devised a plan to lure them out after them. A battle ensued in which many people were slain. However, none of the 2,000 "sons of Helaman^2" were among the dead. They never doubted because they "had been taught by their mothers, that if they did not doubt, God would deliver them" [v. 47].

Alma 57. In the 29th year of the judges, another 60 sons of the Ammonites were added to the 2,000 original band. Helaman^2 and his army sought to retake the city of Cumeni. In doing so, they took so many prisoners that it became necessary to send some, guarded by **Gid** (#113) and a group of soldiers, down to Zarahemla. The prisoners revolted when they overheard some Nephite spies cry out that Lamanite warriors were headed toward Cumeni. A battle ensued and the majority of the prisoners were slain. The rest escaped. Gid and the other guards returned to Cumeni the next day in time to help Helaman^2 and the rest of his army who were under attack from a Lamanite army that had been strengthened by provisions and additional troops sent by Ammoron. Many of Helaman's^2 army were about to give out, but the 2,060 were firm and undaunted. All of the sons of Helaman^2 were injured in the battle, but not one was killed.

Alma 58. The Lord continued to support the sons of Helaman^2. In the 29th year of the reign of the judges, they were with Helaman^2 in the city of Manti. Not one had been slain throughout all of their battles.

111. LAMAN^4

Alma 55:5. <u>LAMAN^4</u> was a **Nephite** (#13) soldier and a descendant of **Laman^1** (#3). [Laman^1 was the eldest son of **Lehi^1** (#1); **Laman^2** (#41) was a Lamanite king about 200 B.C.; **Laman^3** (#42) was the son of Laman^2.] Laman^4 was sought out by **Moroni^1** (#97). Moroni^1 wanted to find a descendant of Laman^1 among his men who could help him in his plan to free the Nephite prisoners and retake the city of Gid from the

Lamanites (#12). It happened that the man they found was also named Laman. He had been one of the servants of the king who fled when the king was murdered by **Amalickiah's** (#99) followers.

Laman[4] and a small group of men approached the Lamanite guards. They tricked them into drinking very strong wine. When the guards were in a drunken sleep, Laman[4] and his men returned and reported to Moroni[1], who was then able to arm the Nephite prisoners and free them, capturing the city of Gid without bloodshed.

112. ANTIPUS

Alma 56:9. **ANTIPUS** had been appointed by **Moroni**[1] (#97) to be a leader over the part of the people that encompassed the city of Judea. **Helaman**[2] (#91) and his 2,000 "sons" joined Antipus to strengthen Antipus's army since it had been reduced by the **Lamanites** (#12). He fell in battle with the Lamanites, along with many of his leaders. Helaman[2] and his 2,000 young sons came to their rescue, and Antipus's remaining warriors rallied. None of Helaman's[2] young warriors were felled in battle.

113. GID

Alma 57:28. **GID** was the **Nephite** (#13) officer appointed by **Helaman**[2] (#91) to be in charge of escorting the **Lamanites** (#12) who were captured in the battle to retain the city of Cumeni to Zarahemla. The prisoners rose in rebellion. Most were slain and the rest escaped. Gid and his men returned to Cumeni just in time to help save Helaman[2] and his sons from being overpowered by the Lamanite army.

Alma 58. He and his band of soldiers, working with Helaman's[2] troops and **Teomner's** (#114) troops, recaptured the city of Manti. This was the 29th year of the judges.

114. TEOMNER

Alma 58:16. **TEOMNER** was a **Nephite** (#13) officer working with **Helaman**[2] (#91) and **Gid** (#113). He and his soldiers took part in recapturing the city of Manti. Helaman's[2] warriors decoyed the **Lamanite**

(#12) army out of the city, and then Gid's and Teomner's armies took the city. Helaman's[2] band headed first in the direction of Zarahemla, but then doubled back to Manti to help hold it.

115. PACHUS

Alma 62:6. <u>PACHUS</u> was the leader of the **king-men** (#106) who rose up against **Pahoran**[1] (#105) and caused him and the **freemen** (#107) to flee from Zarahemla to Gideon. He was killed when **Moroni**[1] (#97) and his army came to Pahoran's[1] aid.

116. MORONIHAH[1]

Alma 62:43. <u>MORONIHAH</u>[1], the son of **Moroni**[1] (#97), took command of the armies in the 32nd year of the reign of the judges when his father retired after restoring peace among the Nephites. [**Moronihah**[2] (#169) was one of the **Nephite** (#13) generals who fell with his 10,000 men in the final great battle.]

Alma 63. The **Lamanites** (#12) waged wars against the army of Moronihah[1] in the 39th year of the judges, but were driven back, suffering great loss.

Helaman 1. In the 41st year of the reign of the judges, **Coriantumr**[3] (#123), an apostate Nephite and leader of the Lamanite army, captured Zarahemla and killed the chief judge **Pacumeni** (#121). Moronihah[1] told **Lehi**[3] (#98) to head off the Lamanite army as they marched to the city of Bountiful, while he headed them off in their retreat. Coriantumr[3] was killed in the ensuing battle. The Nephites regained the city of Zarahemla.

Helaman 4. Moronihah[1] and his armies were driven even into Bountiful. They fortified themselves there against the Lamanites. In the 60th year of the judges, Moronihah[1] and his armies succeeded in regaining many cities from the Lamanites. By the 61st year, they had regained half of all their cities. The Nephite losses were due to their iniquity. Moronihah[1] preached and prophesied to the people and called them to repentance. As they repented, they regained the half of all their possessions. In the 62nd year, they abandoned their efforts to regain more of their possessions because the Lamanites were too strong.

117. HAGOTH

Alma 63:5. <u>HAGOTH</u> was a **Nephite** (#13) ship builder who in the 37th and 38th years of the reign of the judges built many ships for the outward migration that was taking place during those years.

9

People First Mentioned in the Book of Helaman

118.* HELAMAN³ (6)

Alma 63:11. HELAMAN³, son of **Helaman²** (#91), received the sacred records for safekeeping and recording from his uncle **Shiblon** (#92) shortly before Shiblon's death in the 39th year of the reign of the judges [53 B.C.]. [**Helaman¹** (#34) was the son of king **Benjamin** (#30); Helaman², son of **Alma²** (#50), was a prophet and military commander.]

Helaman 2. When **Pacumeni** (#121) was slain by **Coriantumr³** (#123) in the 42nd year of the reign of the judges, Helaman³ was chosen by the people to be the sixth person to fill the judgment-seat. **Gadianton** (#125) plotted to kill him. He sent **Kishkumen** (#122) to do the job. Kishkumen was discovered on his way to commit murder and was killed by Helaman's³ servant. Gadianton and his band went into hiding.

Helaman 3. Helaman³ filled the judgment-seat righteously and walked before God, walking in the ways of his father continually.

From the 43rd year to the 53rd year of the judges, there was mostly peace except for an occasional year when pride caused internal strife among the **Nephites** (#13). During the 46th-48th years, there was a lot of northward migration because of some internal contention.

Helaman's³ sons were **Nephi²** (#127) and **Lehi⁴** (#128). Upon Helaman's³ death in the 53rd year, Nephi² reigned in his stead.

Helaman 5. Prior to Helaman's³ death, he had given his sons some counsel. He reminded them of their "first parents who came out of Jerusalem," after whom they were named, and told them to remember what they stood for. He also counseled them that it is only through the atoning blood of **Christ** (#143) that men can be saved. He also counseled them that Christ is the rock, our Redeemer, upon whom they must build their foundation.

119. PAHORAN² (4)

Helaman 1:3. PAHORAN² was the son of **Pahoran¹** (#105), the third chief judge. Pahoran² was the fourth chief judge. In the 40th year of the judges, he and two of his brothers, **Paanchi** (#120) and **Pacumeni** (#121), contended for the judgment-seat after their father's death. Pahoran² was chosen by the people to be the chief judge and governor over them. Pacumeni joined with the voice of the people. Paanchi rebelled and was condemned to death for rebellion. His followers were angry and sent **Kishkumen** (#122) to kill Pahoran² as he sat on the judgment seat. His brother Pacumeni was then chosen to fill the office.

120. PAANCHI

Helaman 1:3. PAANCHI was one of the sons of **Pahoran¹** (#105) who contended for the judgment-seat upon the death of his father. When his brother **Pahoran²** (#119) was chosen by the people to be chief judge, Paanchi and his followers were angry and sought to lead the people away. Paanchi was tried according to the voice of the people and was condemned to death for rebellion. His followers then sent **Kishkumen** (#122) to kill Pahoran² as he sat on the judgment seat. His brother **Pacumeni** (#121) was then chosen to fill the judgment-seat.

121. PACUMENI (5)

Helaman 1:3. PACUMENI was another son of **Pahoran¹** (#105) who contended for the judgment-seat upon the death of his father. However, when his brother **Pahoran²** (#119) was chosen by the people, Pacumeni united his support with Pahoran's² followers. When **Kishkumen** (#122), one of **Paanchi's** (#120) followers, murdered Pahoran², Pacumeni was appointed by the people "to be a chief judge and a governor" over them to reign in Pahoran's² stead (v. 13).

In the 41st year of the judges, the **Lamanites** (#12), led by **Coriantumr**[3] (#123), captured the city of Zarahemla. Pacumeni tried to flee. He was slain by Coriantumr[3] as he reached the city wall.

122. KISHKUMEN

Helaman 1:9. <u>KISHKUMEN</u> was a murderer and a leader of robbers. In the 40th year of the judges, Kishkumen murdered **Pahoran**[2] (#119) as he sat upon the judgment-seat. Because he was in disguise, no one but those who sent him knew who did it. He and **Paanchi's** (#120) supporters entered into a covenant that they would never reveal Kishkumen's identity.

Helaman 2. Kishkumen was killed by one of **Helaman's**[3] (#118) servants as Kishkumen was on his way to murder Helaman[3] as he sat upon the judgment-seat.

Helaman 6. Kishkumen and **Gadianton** (#125) founded the murderous and evil group called the **Gadianton robbers** (#126).

123. CORIANTUMR[3]

Helaman 1:15. <u>CORIANTUMR</u>[3] was a **Nephite** (#13) dissenter and a descendant of **Zarahemla** (#29). [**Coriantumr**[1] (#197) was an early Jaredite; **Coriantumr**[2] (#232), a Jaredite king, was the last Jaredite survivor.] Coriantumr[3] was a large and mighty man, chosen by the **Lamanite** (#12) king **Tubaloth** (#124) to lead an army into Zarahemla and capture it. He slew the chief judge **Pacumeni** (#121) as he tried to flee. The Lamanite army was taking many cities, killing men, women and children. **Moronihah**[1] (#116) immediately sent **Lehi**[3] (#98) to head off Coriantumr's[3] army before they could reach Bountiful, and he and his army headed them off in their retreat. An exceedingly bloody battle ensued, and Coriantumr[3] was found slain among the dead and wounded. The Nephites once again took possession of the city of Zarahemla, bringing the 41st year of the judges to a close.

124. TUBALOTH

Helaman 1:16. **TUBALOTH** was the son of **Ammoron** (#108). He was the **Lamanite** (#12) king who sent **Coriantumr**[3] (#123) to capture the **Nephite** (#13) city of Zarahemla.

125. GADIANTON

Helaman 2:4. **GADIANTON** was an expert in the craft of murder and robbery. He became the leader of **Kishkumen's** (#122) band. This band was later called the **Gadianton robbers** (#126) and ultimately proved to be the overthrow [almost the entire destruction] of the **Nephite** (#13) civilization.

Helaman 6. Gadianton set up wicked laws for his society. He received the secret oaths and covenants from Satan.

126. GADIANTON ROBBERS

Helaman 2:4. The **GADIANTON ROBBERS** were a murderous group which plundered and carried on the work of darkness. These robbers included many **Nephites** (#13) but even more **Lamanites** (#12) who followed **Gadianton** (#125).

Helaman 6. The Gadianton robbers had secret signs and oaths. Whosoever of their band revealed to the world anything about their wickedness was tried, not according to the laws of the land, but according to their laws of wickedness. Evil ways were revealed to them by Satan. They were responsible for the murders of **Cezoram** (#129) and his **son** (#131) while they sat upon the judgment-seat during the 66th year of the reign of the judges.

By the end of the 62nd year of the reign of the judges [29 B.C.], the majority of the Lamanites had become a righteous people, more so than the Nephites. They preached faith and repentance to the Nephites and told of their conversions. Many of the Lamanites went into the land northward to preach to the people. **Nephi**[2] (#127) and **Lehi**[4] (#128) also went into the land northward to preach. As the Nephites repented, there was peace between the Nephites and Lamanites for a time. By the 68th year of the judges, the Nephites, having prospered, again fell into wickedness while the Lamanites remained true and faithful. The Lamanites hunted out the Gadianton robbers and taught the more wicked part of them, destroying the band in their area [v. 37]. Meanwhile, the Nephites strengthened the Gadianton robbers, allowing them to gain control over their government.

Helaman 7. By the end of the 68th year of the reign of the judges, the Gadianton robbers had taken over the government and even filled the judgment seats [v. 4].

3 Nephi 3. The Gadianton robbers under Giddianhi (#138) gave Lachoneus[1] (#136) an order to submit everything to them or be destroyed in battle [A.D. 15]. Lachoneus[1] appointed Gidgiddoni (#139) to lead the Nephite armies.

3 Nephi 4. The Gadianton robbers were defeated. Giddianhi, chief of the Gadianton robbers, was slain. His successor, Zemnarihah (#140), was hanged [v 28].

127.* NEPHI[2] (7)

Helaman 3:21. **NEPHI[2],** older son of **Helaman[3]** (#118) and brother to **Lehi[4]** (#128), became the seventh chief judge. The judgment-seat was passed on to him when his father died in the 53rd year of the judges. [**Nephi[1]** (#6), fourth son of **Lehi[1]** (#1), was a great prophet. His posterity and those who followed him were called **Nephites** (#13); **Nephi[3]** (#137), the son of Nephi[2], was one of the twelve Nephite disciples chosen by Jesus; **Nephi[4]** (#155), son of Nephi[3], kept the records.]

Helaman 4. During the 43rd through the 56th years of the judges, there was peace between the Nephites and the **Lamanites** (#12). However, the Nephites were again becoming proud and wicked, and Nephite dissenters joined the Lamanites and stirred them to battle, and they did commence the work of death [v. 5] in the 57th year. During the 57th through the 59th years, the Nephites lost much land. But, during the 60th-61st years of the judges, **Moronihah[1]** (#116) succeeded with his armies in recapturing half of the land they had lost. Nephi[2], Lehi[4] and Moronihah[1] preached and prophesied to the people and called them to repentance. As they repented, they regained half of their lands. At the end of the 62nd year, they gave up trying to regain any more land because of the strength of the Lamanites.

Helaman 5. In the 62nd year of the reign of the judges, Nephi[2] gave up the judgment-seat to **Cezoram** (#129). Those who chose evil were now more numerous than those who chose righteousness. The laws had been corrupted and the people were ripening for destruction. Nephi[2] and Lehi[4] spent the rest of their lives preaching the gospel.

Nephi[2] and Lehi[4] were powerful missionaries. They not only preached to the Nephites, but also to the Lamanites. Eight thousand Lamanites in Zarahemla were converted. In the land of Nephi, however, Nephi[2] and Lehi[4] were cast into prison, the same one into which **Ammon**[2] (#51) and his brethren had been cast by the servants of **Limhi** (#39). Nephi[2] and Lehi[4] were kept without food for many days. When the people (apparently about 300 strong) came to get them to slay them, Nephi[2] and Lehi[4] were encircled about as if by fire. The walls of the prison shook and the earth trembled and a voice from heaven spoke to those Lamanites and Nephite dissenters who were there and were surrounded by a cloud of darkness. One Nephite dissenter, **Aminadab** (#130), a former member of the church, explained to those with him who it was who was speaking and told them they must all repent in order to remove the cloud of darkness. When they cried unto God, they found themselves, everyone, encircled about by a pillar of fire. Marvelous things occurred: the Holy Spirit of God came down and entered their hearts; they could speak marvelous things; a voice spoke to them saying, "Peace, peace be unto you, because of your faith in my Well Beloved, who was from the foundation of the world" [v.47]; they saw the heavens open and angels came down out of heaven and ministered unto them.

These Lamanites and former Nephites then also preached unto the people, and the greater part of the people were converted; they gave the Nephites' lands back to them.

Helaman 6. Nephi[2] and Lehi[4] went to the land northward to preach. The 63rd year ended [v. 6]. In the 66th year of the judges, Cezoram and

Cezoram's son (#131), the eighth and ninth chief judges, were murdered by members of **Gadianton's band** (#126). By the 68th year, the Nephites had become extremely wicked while the Lamanites grew in righteousness, destroying Gadianton's band from among their people.

Helaman 7. By the end of the 68th year of the reign of the judges [24 B.C.], wickedness prevailed and the Gadianton robbers controlled the government and occupied the judgment-seats. Nephi[2] returned from preaching in the land northward where he was rejected. Seeing the wickedness of the people, he cried out to God in despair. People passing along the road saw him in his garden tower and heard his lament. They ran and told others and a large group assembled. Nephi[2] chastised them and told them to repent.

Helaman 8. Corrupt judges sought to turn the people against Nephi[2]. As he spoke to them, he told them that their chief judge **Seezoram** (#133) had been murdered by his own brother **Seantum** (#134), who wanted the judgment-seat for himself. He further told them that they both belonged to Gadianton's band.

Helaman 9. Five messengers were sent to verify Nephi's[2] words. They were taken prisoner and blamed for the murder. When the people gathered the next day for the burial of their chief judge, those who had heard Nephi[2] the previous day inquired about the five messengers. When the people brought the prisoners before the judges, they recognized them as the five messengers. The judges then decided to blame Nephi[2] for the death and bound him and brought him before the people. Nephi[2] chastised them and told them to go the house of Seantum and that Seantum would ultimately confess to the murder. Many of those who heard Nephi[2] were converted.

Helaman 10. Nephi[2] was given the sealing power by the Lord and told that "all things shall be done unto thee according to thy word, for thou shalt not ask that which is contrary to my will" [v. 5]. He was carried by the Spirit from multitude to multitude and the people could not take him to cast him into prison. Thus ended the 71st year of the judges.

Helaman 11. In the 72nd year [20 B.C.] wickedness increased and there were wars throughout the land. According to Nephi's[2] word, famine covered the land during the 73rd to the 76th years. In the 76th year, the people repented, and Nephi[2] prayed that the famine might be ended, and it was so. Beginning in the 76th year and continuing through the 79th year of the judges, the people prospered. A few doctrinal concerns were settled in the 78th year and more in the 79th. War between the Lamanites and Nephite dissenters and their brethren erupted in the 80th year [12 B.C.]. The Gadianton band was revived once more. By the end of the 85th year [7 B.C.], the people were ripening again for destruction.

Helaman 13-15. **Samuel[2] the Lamanite** (#135) prophesied of the signs surrounding the birth and also the death of **Jesus Christ** (#143), and told the people of their destruction if they didn't repent.

Helaman 16. The Nephites who believed Samuel[2] sought out Nephi[2] and were baptized. During this time, the 86th year of the reign of the judges, he was baptizing, prophesying, preaching, showing signs and wonders, and working miracles among the people.

3 Nephi 1. The 91st year of the reign of the judges had passed, marking 600 years from the time that **Lehi[1]** (#1) and his family left Jerusalem. **Nephi[2]** departed out of the land, leaving his son **Nephi[3]** (#137) in charge of the records. Nephi[2] was not heard of again.

128. LEHI[4]

Helaman 3:21. <u>LEHI[4]</u>, brother of **Nephi[2]** (#127), was the younger son of **Helaman[3]** (#118). [**Lehi[1]** (#1), a Hebrew prophet, led his family and other followers out from Jerusalem to the Americas; **Lehi[2]** (#72) and **Lehi[3]** (#98) may be one and the same person, according to the Index to The Book of Mormon. Lehi[3] was a Nephite military commander.]

During the 43rd through the 56th years of the judges, there was peace between the **Nephites** (#13) and the **Lamanites** (#12). However, the Nephites were again becoming proud and wicked, and Nephite dissenters joined the Lamanites and stirred them into battle. During the 57th-59th years, the Nephites lost much land. In the 60th-61st years of the judges, **Moronihah**[1] (#116) and his armies recaptured half of the Nephite lands. Lehi[4], Nephi[2] and Moronihah[1] preached and prophesied to the people and called them to repentance. As they repented, they regained half of their lands. At the end of the 62nd year, they gave up trying to regain any more land because of the strength of the Lamanites.

Helaman 5. In the 62nd year of the reign of the judges, Nephi[2] gave up the judgment-seat to **Cezoram** (#129). Those who chose evil were now more numerous than those who chose righteousness. The laws had been corrupted and the people were ripening for destruction. Lehi[4] and Nephi[2] spent the rest of their lives preaching the gospel.

Lehi[4] and Nephi[2] were powerful missionaries. They not only preached to the Nephites but also to the Lamanites. Eight thousand Lamanites in Zarahemla were converted. In the land of Nephi, however, Lehi[4] and Nephi[2] were cast into prison, the same one into which **Ammon**[2] (#51) and his brethren had been cast by the servants of **Limhi** (#39). Lehi[4] and Nephi[2] were kept without food for many days. When the people (apparently about 300 strong) came to slay them, Lehi[4] and Nephi[2] were encircled about as if by fire. The walls of the prison shook and the earth trembled. A cloud of darkness surrounded those Lamanites and Nephite dissenters who were there. A voice from heaven spoke to them. One Nephite dissenter, **Aminadab** (#130), a former member of the church, explained to the others that God was speaking and told them they must all repent and cry unto the voice, even until ye shall have faith in Christ, in order to remove the cloud of darkness [v. 41]. When they did, they found themselves, everyone, encircled about by a pillar of fire. Marvelous things occurred: the Holy Spirit of God came down and entered their hearts; they could speak marvelous things; a voice spoke to them saying, "Peace, peace be unto you, because of your faith in my Well Beloved, who was from the foundation of the world" [v. 47]; they saw the heavens open and angels came down out of heaven and ministered unto them.

These Lamanites and Nephites began preaching unto the people and the greater part of the people were converted. They then gave the Nephites' lands back to them.

Helaman 6. Many Lamanites went into the land northward to preach to the people. Lehi[4] and Nephi[2] also went into the land northward to preach. The 63rd year ended [v. 6].

Helaman 11. Nephi[2] was esteemed by the people "as a great prophet, and a man of God, having great power and authority given unto him from God. And behold, Lehi, his brother, was not a whit behind him as to things pertaining to righteousness" [vs. 18-19]. Lehi[4], Nephi[2], and many of their brethren, had revelations daily.

129. CEZORAM (8)

Helaman 5:1. **CEZORAM** became the eighth chief judge. In the 62nd year of the reign of the judges [30 B.C.], **Nephi[2]** (#127) gave up the judgment-seat to Cezoram. Those who chose evil were now more numerous than those who chose righteousness. The laws had been corrupted, and the people were ripening for destruction.

Helaman 6. Nephi[2] and **Lehi[4]** (#128) had much success as they preached among the Lamanites, and by the end of the 62nd year, the **Lamanites** (#12) were more righteous than the **Nephites** (#13). In the 63rd through the 65th years, the Nephites and Lamanites were at peace. They had free trade between them, and they prospered greatly. In the 66th year [26 B.C.], Cezoram was murdered as he sat upon the judgment-seat and so was **Cezoram's son** (#131) who followed him in that position. The unknown assailant was a member of **Gadianton's robbers** (#126) and murderers. The greater part of the Nephites now belonged to this band.

130. AMINADAB

Helaman 5:39. **AMINADAB,** an apostate **Nephite** (#13), was with the crowd of 300 people who heard and saw marvelous things when they went to get **Nephi[2]** (#127) and **Lehi[4]** (#128) from prison to slay them. As a former member of the church, he was able to explain to the **Lamanites** (#12) and the Nephite dissenters that in order to get rid of the dark cloud they had to repent. The people did so, and they saw and heard many marvelous things. They were surrounded as if by fire, and the heavens opened and angels came down and administered to them. The

Spirit of the Lord filled them and a voice from heaven spoke to them. After this marvelous experience, those present were converted and went about preaching.

131. CEZORAM'S SON (9)

Helaman 6:15. <u>CEZORAM'S SON</u> was appointed by the people to be the ninth chief judge when **Cezoram** (#129) was murdered. He was also murdered by someone from **Gadianton's band** (#126) that same year as he sat upon the judgment-seat.

132. EZIAS

Helaman 8:20. <u>EZIAS,</u> a prophet known by the **Nephites** (#13), testified of **Christ** (#143).

133. SEEZORAM (10)

Helaman 9:23. <u>SEEZORAM</u> was the tenth chief judge and the one **Nephi**[2] (#127) referred to in Helaman 8:27. He was murdered by his brother **Seantum** (#134), who wanted to be chief judge himself. Both men were members of the **Gadianton robbers** (#126).

134. SEANTUM

Helaman 9:25. <u>SEANTUM</u> killed his brother **Seezoram** (#133) as he sat on the judgment-seat because he wanted the judgment-seat for himself. **Nephi**[2] (#127) revealed both the murder and the murderer to the crowd when they gathered around him as he cried out his soul upon the tower in his garden. He gave a sign unto the people and prophesied that Seantum would first deny and then ultimately confess to the murder of his brother. Both Seezoram and Seantum were members of **Gadianton's robbers** (#126). The years were between 23 B.C. and 20 B.C.

135. SAMUEL[2]

Helaman 13:2. <u>SAMUEL</u>[2] or <u>"SAMUEL THE LAMANITE"</u> preached to the **Nephites** (#13) and was rejected by them. [**Samuel**[1]

(SA #30) was a Hebrew prophet.] As Samuel[2] the Lamanite left to return to his own land, the Lord instructed him to return and preach whatsoever should come into his heart to say to the Nephites. Because they would not let him into the city of Zarahemla, he climbed upon the city wall and preached from there. He prophesied that 400 years would not pass away before the people would be smitten with famine, pestilence and the sword, and be destroyed. There would be those of the fourth generation of their enemies who would live to witness their destruction. Their riches would be cursed and become slippery.

Helaman 14. Samuel[2] prophesied that in five years the sign would be given indicating the birth of the **Savior** (#143): great lights in heaven, no darkness for a day and a night and a day, a new star would arise, and there would be many signs and wonders in heaven.

He also told them the signs to watch for which would indicate the Savior's death: the sun would be darkened and also the moon and the stars, and there would be no light upon the face of that land for the space of three days; there would be thunderings and lightnings for the space of many hours at the time Christ yields up the ghost; there would be earthquakes and tempests, and mountains would be laid low and valleys would become mountains; highways would be broken up and cities would become desolate; and many graves would be opened.

Helaman 15. Samuel[2] reminded the Nephites of how the Lord had blessed them, but they had turned away. The **Lamanites** (#12), on the other hand, were being more and more righteous. They even buried their weapons and would suffer themselves to be slain rather than fight again. He also reminded the Nephites that the Lord had promised to be merciful to the Lamanites in the latter days. He also reminded them that if the Lamanites had had the mighty works shown unto them that had been shown unto the Nephites, the Lamanites would never again have dwindled in unbelief.

Helaman 16. Those who believed Samuel[2] sought out **Nephi**[2] (#127) and were baptized. The majority tried to slay Samuel[2]. He fled unto his own people and preached and prophesied among them and was never heard of again among the Nephites. Thus, the 86th year of the judges ended.

10

People First Mentioned in the Book of 3 Nephi

136. LACHONEUS[1] (11?)

3 Nephi 1:1. <u>LACHONEUS[1]</u> was a righteous Nephite chief judge and governor over the land at the end of the 91st year of the reign of the judges. Six hundred years had passed since **Lehi[1]** (#1) left Jerusalem. [**Lachoneus[2]** (#141) was his son.] *Note:* The scriptures say that Lachoneus[1] was chief judge at the time the 91st year had passed away. However, it is not clear as to when he became chief judge, nor is it clear who was chief judge between 20 B.C. when **Seezoram** (#133) was chief judge and A.D. 1. We are just told that when the 91st year had passed away, Lachoneus[1] was chief judge. Since no other chief judge is named between Seezoram and Lachoneus[1], he was most likely the 11th chief judge.

3 Nephi 3. When **Giddianhi** (#138) sent him an epistle demanding that the **Nephites** (#13) give all they had to his band of **Gadianton robbers** (#126) and then join them, Lachoneus[1] sent a proclamation throughout all his land. He gathered the people together at Zarahemla, called them to repentance, strengthened them, and prepared them for when Giddianhi and his robbers would come against them. He also appointed chief captains over all his armies. The chiefest of these was **Gidgiddoni** (#139).

3 Nephi 6. By the end of the 26th and 27th years A.D., peace had been reestablished through the efforts of Lachoneus[1], Gidgiddoni, and the other leaders who had been appointed over the people. In the 31st year, the judgment-seat was passed on to Lachoneus[2], and the people in that year willfully rebelled against God.

137.* NEPHI³

3 Nephi 1:2. **NEPHI³** was the father of **Nephi⁴** (#155) and the eldest son of **Nephi²** (#127). [**Nephi¹** (#6), the fourth son of **Lehi¹** (#1), was a great prophet and founder of the Nephite nation. Nephi² was a great missionary son of **Helaman³** (#118).] In the 91st year of the reign of the judges, 600 years from when Lehi¹ and his family left Jerusalem, the records were passed on from Nephi² to his son Nephi³. Nephi² then left the land, never to be heard of again.

The prophecies pertaining to the birth of the **Savior** (#143) began to be fulfilled in the 92nd year [A.D. 1]. The non-believers had designated a day when all believers would be put to death unless the prophecies were fulfilled by then. With a sorrowful heart because of the wickedness of the people, Nephi³ prayed all day long to the Lord and finally received the answer that the sign would be given that very night. The Savior would be born "on the morrow." After the signs were given, many people believed, and Nephi³ and others went throughout the land preaching and baptizing.

During the 93rd year [A.D. 2] and 94th year [A.D. 3], the **Gadianton robbers** (#126) increased their influence, and many of the younger generation were led away.

3 Nephi 2. The people began to forget the signs and wonders they had heard and seen. The years A.D. 4 through A.D. 15 saw wickedness increase so much that by A.D. 13 the righteous were threatened with total destruction by the Gadianton robbers. The righteous **Lamanites** (#12) and **Nephites** (#13) all came together for protection. The curse was taken from the righteous Lamanites, and their skin became white like the Nephites.

The Nephites began to reckon time from when the sign of the Savior's birth was given. The 92nd year of the judges was A.D.1.

3 Nephi 5. Nephi³ recorded his record on the plates of Nephi which **Mormon²** (#159) later abridged.

3 Nephi 7. During A.D. 31 and A.D. 32, Nephi[3], having been visited by angels and also by the voice of the Lord, preached boldly among the people and called them to repentance. The people were angry with him. Nevertheless, in the name of Jesus, he cast out devils and unclean spirits and raised his brother **Timothy** (#144) from the dead after he had been stoned to death by the people. He ordained many people to the ministry, and in the commencement of the 33rd year, many of the people were baptized unto repentance.

3 Nephi 11. In A.D. 34, when Jesus appeared to the Nephites, he called Nephi[3] and others forward and gave them power to baptize after the Savior's ascension again into heaven.

3 Nephi 19:4. Nephi[3] was called by Jesus to be one of the twelve disciples. Nephi[3] went down into the water and was baptized. When he came out of the water, he baptized others, including all the other eleven disciples chosen by the Savior. After they were all baptized, the Holy Ghost fell upon all of them.

3 Nephi 23. The Savior had Nephi[3] bring the record forth. He reminded them that **Samuel**[2] **the Lamanite** (#135) had prophesied that in the day the Father glorified his name in Jesus Christ, many saints would rise from the dead and minister unto the people. He then asked why the fulfillment of that prophecy had not been recorded. He then commanded Nephi[3] to record it, which he did.

138. GIDDIANHI

3 Nephi 3:1, 9. **GIDDIANHI** was the leader and governor of the **Gadianton robbers** (#126) in A.D. 16. He sent an epistle to **Lachoneus**[1] (#136) demanding that the **Nephites** (#13) give them all their lands and possessions and join them or be destroyed in battle.

3 Nephi 4. In the sixth month of the nineteenth year, he sent his robbers to battle the Nephites. It was the worst battle in terms of casualties since **Lehi**[1] (#1) left Jerusalem. The Nephites were victorious, and Giddianhi was slain. He was succeeded by **Zemnarihah** (#140).

139. GIDGIDDONI

3 Nephi 3:18. <u>GIDGIDDONI</u> was appointed chiefest of the chief commanders and the great commander of all the **Nephite** (#13) armies by **Lachoneus**[1] (#136) in A.D. 17. He was a prophet as well as the chief commander since it was the custom of the people to appoint someone to that position who had the spirit of prophecy. Gidgiddoni had the people make weapons of war of every kind, and strong armor, shields and bucklers. He told the people that they should not go out after the robbers but should wait in their own land to defend themselves, and the Lord would be with them.

3 Nephi 4. Under Gidgiddoni's command, **Giddianhi** (#138), the leader of the **Gadianton robbers** (#126), was slain in battle. **Zemnarihah** (#140), Giddianhi's successor, did not come up to battle against the Nephites, but he had his robbers lay siege on all sides of them. However, the Nephites marched out by day and by night and fell upon the robbers. Zemnarihah decided to have his people retreat because of hunger and loss of people. Gidgiddoni had his men at night march beyond the robbers and surround them. As the robbers withdrew, many were captured and the remainder were slain. Zemnarihah was captured and hanged from a tree. The Nephites repented of all their sins and abominations and served God diligently.

3 Nephi 6. Gidgiddoni, along with Lachoneus[1] and the other leaders who had been appointed over the people, established peace in the land.

140. ZEMNARIHAH

3 Nephi 4:17. <u>ZEMNARIHAH</u> was the leader and governor of the **Gadianton robbers** (#126) during A.D. 19-21. He did not come up to battle against the **Nephites** (#13), but he had his robbers lay siege on all sides of the Nephites. However, the Nephites marched out by day and by night and fell upon the robbers. Zemnarihah decided to have his people retreat because of hunger and loss of people. **Gidgiddoni** (#139) had his men at night march beyond the robbers and surround them. As the robbers withdrew, many were captured and the remainder were slain. Zemnarihah was captured and hanged from a tree.

141. LACHONEUS² (Last Chief Judge)

3 Nephi 6:19. **LACHONEUS²,** the son of **Lachoneus¹** (#136), filled the judgment-seat and governorship after his father [A.D. 29-30]. During the 30th year, the people grew very wicked, even those who had been high priests and lawyers, and they secretly killed the prophets contrary to the law of the land. They set the laws of the land at defiance and sought to be subject to kings again.

3 Nephi 7. It was in this same year that Lachoneus², the chief judge of the land, was murdered and the people were divided one from another into separate tribes. The government was destroyed, ending the period of the judges.

142. JACOB⁴

3 Nephi 7:9. **JACOB⁴** was a wicked apostate **Nephite** (#13) chosen king by the secret combination group that destroyed the government of the land [A.D. 30]. He was one of the chiefest who had spoken against the prophets. [**Jacob¹** (SA #8) is father of the twelve tribes of Israel, see the Old Testament; **Jacob²** (#10) was the son of **Lehi¹** (#1); **Jacob³** (#109) was a Nephite apostate of the **Zoramite²** (#89) sect.]

3 Nephi 9. Because of the wickedness of the inhabitants of the city of Jacobugath, that city was burned when the **Savior** (#143) was crucified.

143. JESUS CHRIST
(3 Nephi 8 thru 30)

3 Nephi 8. **JESUS CHRIST** is also referred to as the **REDEEMER,** the **GOOD SHEPHERD**, the **LORD**, and the **SAVIOR.** The signs which prophets had said would accompany the Savior's death began to be fulfilled on the fourth day of the first month of the 34th year A.D. There were earthquakes and terrible tempests and thunder, cities were burned, other cities were buried in the depths of the sea or swallowed up by the land. High places were made low, and low places were made high. All this occurred in the space of about three hours. Then there was terrible darkness for three days.

3 Nephi 9. During this time, the voice of the Savior was heard among the inhabitants. The Savior told of the extent of the destruction and why some cities were destroyed. He proclaimed his divinity and announced that the law of Moses was fulfilled in him and that burnt offerings were done away and would no longer be accepted by him. The only acceptable sacrifice would now be a broken heart and a contrite spirit [vs. 19-20]. He invited all to come unto him and be saved.

3 Nephi 10. The people were astonished. There was silence in the land for the space of many hours.

The voice came a second time. Jesus Christ reminded the people that he had often gathered his children together as a mother hen gathereth her chicks, and how oft he would have gathered them, but they would not. Those who were preserved from the destruction were the more righteous part of the people—those who had received the prophets and had not stoned them nor had shed the blood of the saints.

In the ending of the 34th year, the people had great favors shown unto them, and great blessings were poured out upon their heads. Soon after the ascension of Christ into heaven, he appeared unto those Nephites and Lamanites who had been spared.

3 Nephi 11. A large group of people were gathered around the temple in Bountiful. As they were marveling and discussing Jesus Christ, a voice was heard from heaven, but they could not understand it.

They heard the voice a second time, and still did not understand it.

The voice came a third time, and this time they understood it. The Father said: "Behold my Beloved Son, in whom I am well pleased, in whom I have glorified my name—hear ye him" [v. 7]. Jesus then came down from heaven and proclaimed his atonement. One by one, the people thrust their hands in his side and felt the prints of the nails in his hands and feet. The people fell down and worshipped the Lord.

Jesus called **Nephi**[3] (#137) forward and gave him power to baptize the people after he, the Savior, returned to heaven. He also called others and gave power unto them to do likewise. He instructed them as to the correct procedure to follow and the words to say. Contention is not of the Lord, but is of the devil. The Savior's doctrine is that men must believe in him, repent and be baptized, receive the Holy Ghost and become as little children.

3 Nephi 12. The number Christ called and commissioned was twelve. They are listed by name in 3 Nephi 19. He delivered the Beatitudes in a discourse similar to the Sermon on the Mount. His teachings fulfill and take precedence over the law of Moses. Men are commanded to become perfect even as Jesus and the Father in Heaven are perfect.

3 Nephi 13. The Savior continued to preach to the people. He instructed them regarding prayer and fasting and taught them the Lord's prayer. Other messages included: lay not up treasures on earth, but in heaven; have an eye single to the glory of God; no man can serve two masters. To his newly chosen disciples, he counseled, "Take no thought for your life, what ye shall eat, or what ye shall drink; nor yet for your body, what ye shall put on . . . " or for other temporal things for "your heavenly Father knoweth that ye have need of all these things" [vs. 25-32].

3 Nephi 14. Jesus taught the people to not judge others; to not cast pearls before swine; to ask and it shall be given; to do unto others as they would be done to; to enter in at the strait gate; to beware of false prophets; and that he who doeth the will of the Lord is like a man who built his house upon a rock.

3 Nephi 15. Jesus said he had come to fulfill the law of Moses. They, the people to whom he was then speaking, are the "other sheep" to whom he referred in Jerusalem. However, because of wickedness, those in Jerusalem did not understand. There are also other sheep in other places.

3 Nephi 16. Jesus told the people that he had been commanded by the Father to show himself unto the other sheep, those to whom he had never revealed himself thus far. In the latter days, the gospel will go forth first to the Gentiles and then to the house of Israel. All will see eye to eye when he brings again Zion.

3 Nephi 17. As Jesus prepared to leave, saying he would return on the morrow, the people longed for him to stay. He had them bring their sick and lame, and he healed them. He prayed for the people as they all knelt together, "and no tongue can speak, neither can there be written by any man" [v. 17] the things he said, so marvelous were they. He blessed the little children and the heavens opened and angels came down and ministered unto them, encircling them about with fire. There were about 2,500 people there at the time.

3 Nephi 18. Jesus instituted the sacrament, giving the bread and wine to his twelve disciples and having them, in turn, give to the multitude. They were commanded to always follow the specific procedure and give the sacrament to those who were baptized into the church. They must watch and pray always, praying to the Father in the name of Jesus individually, in their families, and in church. Those who eat and drink of his flesh and blood unworthily are damned. Nevertheless, no one should be cast out from the synagogue; everyone should be made welcome. He touched the disciples and gave them power to confer the Holy Ghost. He then ascended to heaven shielded by a cloud from the view of the masses but not from the view of the disciples [vs. 38- 39].

3 Nephi 19. Word was spread throughout the night that Jesus would return the next day. Thus, a huge crowd assembled, so huge that the twelve disciples divided it into twelve sections, and each disciple taught a group. The twelve disciples were baptized, beginning with Nephi[3], who in turn baptized the other eleven. They received the Holy Ghost and were ministered to by angels and were surrounded by fire. Jesus appeared in their midst. He prayed for them three times, all the while the disciples were praying. His words were so marvelous they cannot be written. The faith of the people was greater than it ever was among the Jews; thus, they saw things the Jews never did.

The twelve disciples were Nephi[3] and his brother **Timothy** (#144), whom Nephi[3] had raised from the dead; **Jonas**[1] (#145), son of Nephi[3]; **Mathoni** (#146) and his brother **Mathonihah** (#147); **Kumen** (#148); **Kumenonhi** (#149); **Jeremiah**[2] (#150); **Shemnon** (#151); **Jonas**[2] (#152); **Zedekiah**[2] (#153) and **Isaiah**[2] (#154).

PEOPLE FIRST MENTIONED IN 3 NEPHI

141

3 Nephi 20. Jesus again administered the sacrament, miraculously providing the bread and wine. The remnant of **Jacob**[1] (SA #8) shall come to the knowledge of the Lord, and they will inherit the Americas and their promised land. Jesus is the prophet to whom **Moses** (SA #2) referred when he said, "A prophet shall the Lord your God raise up unto you of your brethren, like unto me . . . " [v. 23]. Other tribes of the house of Israel will be gathered to Jerusalem.

3 Nephi 21. Jesus gave a sign unto the people that they might know when the Father's promises to the house of Israel were to be fulfilled. This was the sign: Israel will be gathered when these things [The Book of Mormon] come forth. It will be brought forth by the Gentiles and carried to the house of Israel by them. America was set up as a free people by the power of the Father so that The Book of Mormon could come forth unto his covenant people. If the Gentiles believe and obey, they will be saved and counted among the house of Jacob[1]; if not, they will be destroyed. Israel shall build up the New Jerusalem assisted by the Gentiles, and the lost tribes will be gathered to the land of their inheritance.

3 Nephi 22. Jesus quoted Isaiah 54.

3 Nephi 23. Jesus commended the words of **Isaiah**[1] (SA #11) to the people and told them to search the words of the prophets. He instructed them to write the things he had told them. He chastised them for not having recorded the fulfillment of the prophecy of **Samuel**[2] **the Lamanite** (#135) concerning the resurrection of others and commanded them to record it.

3 Nephi 24. He gave them the words the Father gave unto **Malachi** (SA #31) regarding the Lord's messenger who would prepare the way for the Second Coming and commanded them to write them. Christ will sit in judgment. They were commanded to pay tithes and offerings. A book of remembrance was written.

3 Nephi 25. The proud and wicked shall be burned as stubble at the Second Coming. **Elijah** (SA #33) shall return before that great and terrible day and turn the hearts of the fathers to their children and the hearts of the children to their fathers.

3 Nephi 26. Jesus expounded all things from the beginning to the end when he would come in his glory. People will be judged of their works; if good, to the resurrection of everlasting life; if evil, to the resurrection of damnation. [**Mormon**[2] (#159) interrupted this narrative to explain that this book only contains a fraction of the record. The greater part was written on the plates of Nephi. This part was to be given to the people to try their faith. If they believe, greater things would be made manifest unto them.]

The Savior taught the people for three days, and then visited them and taught them often after that. He ministered unto the children, and the children spake marvelous things, such that the people were forbidden to write them.

The disciples taught and baptized from this time on. Those they baptized were called the church of Christ. The people had all things in common.

3 Nephi 27. The Savior told his disciples that everything they do should be done in his name, including calling the church by his name and praying to the Father in his name. His gospel is: that he came into the world to do the will of the Father, to be lifted up upon the cross that he might draw all men unto him, that they should be lifted up by the Father to stand before the Savior and be judged of their works. People must repent and be baptized. No unclean thing can enter his kingdom. They were told to do those things they had seen him do. They were told to keep a record, for out of the books shall the people be judged. None of this generation would be lost, but the fourth generation would be led away.

3 Nephi 28. Nine of the disciples desired that after they had lived to the age of man, they be allowed to come unto Jesus in his kingdom. He told them that after they reached the age of 72, they would come unto him. The other three disciples desired to remain on the earth until Jesus again comes in glory. He granted them their wish. Thus, their bodies underwent a change, not equal to that which shall take place at the last day, but a change such that Satan could have no power over them and they could remain on the earth without tasting death. Mormon[2] was forbidden to reveal their names, but indicated he had seen them, and they had ministered unto him.

3 Nephi 29. The coming forth of The Book of Mormon will signal that the Lord has commenced gathering Israel in fulfillment of his covenants. "Wo unto him that spurneth at the doings of the Lord" [v. 5].

3 Nephi 30. The Gentiles are called to repentance and invited to be numbered with the house of Israel. And the 34th year passed away.

THE SAVIOR'S TWELVE DISCIPLES IN AMERICA
(#'s 137, 144 thru 154)

(137.) NEPHI³

3 Nephi 19:4. NEPHI³ was the first and chief disciple of the twelve Nephite disciples.

144. TIMOTHY

3 Nephi 19:4. TIMOTHY was **Nephi's³** (#137) brother and was one of the twelve Nephite disciples. Nephi³ had once raised him from the dead.

145. JONAS¹

3 Nephi 19:4. JONAS¹ was **Nephi's³** (#137) son and was one of the twelve Nephite disciples. [**Jonas²** (#152) was another disciple.]

146. MATHONI

3 Nephi 19:4. MATHONI was one of the twelve Nephite disciples.

147. MATHONIHAH

3 Nephi 19:4. MATHONIHAH, the brother of Mathoni (#146), was one of the twelve Nephite disciples.

148. KUMEN

3 Nephi 19:4. <u>KUMEN</u> was one of the twelve Nephite disciples.

149. KUMENONHI

3 Nephi 19:4. <u>KUMENONHI</u> was one of the twelve Nephite disciples.

150. JEREMIAH[2]

3 Nephi 19:4. <u>JEREMIAH</u>[2] was one of the twelve Nephite disciples. [**Jeremiah**[1] (SA #6) was a Hebrew prophet, a contemporary of **Lehi**[1] (#1) at the time Lehi[1] and his family left Jerusalem in 600 B.C.]

151. SHEMNON

3 Nephi 19:4. <u>SHEMNON</u> was one of the twelve Nephite disciples.

152. JONAS[2]

3 Nephi 19:4. <u>JONAS</u>[2] was one of the twelve Nephite disciples. [**Jonas**[1] (#145), the son of Nephi[3] (#137), was also a Nephite disciple.]

153. ZEDEKIAH[2]

3 Nephi 19:4. <u>ZEDEKIAH</u>[2] was one of the twelve Nephite disciples. [**Zedekiah**[1] (SA #1) was the last king of Judah around 600 B.C.]

154. ISAIAH[2]

3 Nephi 19:4. <u>ISAIAH</u>[2] was one of the twelve Nephite disciples. [**Isaiah**[1] (SA #11) was a Hebrew prophet around the eighth century B.C., whose writings are recorded in the Old Testament and who is quoted by the Savior and Book of Mormon prophets.]

11

People First Mentioned in the Book of 4 Nephi

155.* NEPHI[4]

Heading. <u>NEPHI</u>[4] was the son of **Nephi**[3] (#137). [Nephi[3] was the chief disciple called by Jesus. **Nephi**[1] (#6) was the fourth son of **Lehi**[1] (#1) and **Sariah** (#2) and was a prophet and founder of the Nephite nation; **Nephi**[2] (#127), the son of **Helaman**[3] (#118), was a great Nephite missionary.] There was peace in the land during Nephi's[4] time, including the years from A.D. 34 through A.D. 110. By A.D. 100, all of the disciples called by Jesus had passed away except the three who were promised they could remain on earth, and new disciples had been called in their stead.

4 Nephi 1. Nephi[4] kept the record on the plates of Nephi. Upon his death, his son **Amos**[1] (#156) kept the record.

156.* AMOS[1]

4 Nephi 1:19. <u>AMOS</u>[1], son of **Nephi**[4] (#155), was the father of **Amos**[2] (#157). By A.D. 110, Nephi[4] had died, and Amos[1] became the keeper of the record. He kept the record for 84 years, during which time there was peace in the land. However, a small band of people revolted from the church and again took upon themselves the name of **Lamanites** (#12). Amos[1] died in A.D. 194, and his son Amos[2] became the keeper of the record.

157.* AMOS[2]

4 Nephi 1:21. <u>AMOS</u>[2], the son of **Amos**[1] (#156), became keeper of the records in A.D. 194 and kept them for an undermined period. By the year 201, all the second generation had passed away save a very few. The people had multiplied greatly upon the land. The people again began to be lifted up in pride. They no longer had their goods and substance in common, and they began to deny the true church of **Christ** (#143). By A.D. 211 there were many churches and all manner of wickedness. The members of the true church were persecuted by those who belonged to another church which denied Christ. By A.D. 231, they had dwindled in wickedness and unbelief and a great division occurred among the people, giving rise once again to **Nephites** (#13) and **Lamanites** (#12). By A.D. 244, the wicked part of the people were exceedingly more numerous than were the people of God. By A.D. 301, both the Lamanites and the Nephites had become exceedingly wicked and the **Gadianton robbers** (#126) had spread over the face of the land. There were none righteous save the disciples of Jesus. Amos[2] died A.D. 306 and his brother **Ammaron** (#158) kept the record.

158.* AMMARON

4 Nephi 1:47. **AMMARON** was the brother of **Amos**. Ammaron became the keeper of the records when Amos died. Who this Amos was is uncertain. Amos[2] had received the plates in A.D. 194 (4 Nephi 1:21); the Amos from whom Ammaron received the plates died in A.D. 305, 112 years later. There may have been several generations in between, and the time span appears too great to assume that Ammaron received the plates from Amos[2]. Because the people were so wicked by A.D. 321, the Holy Ghost constrained him to hide up the sacred records.

Mormon 1. About the time Ammaron hid up the record, he approached **Mormon**[2] (#159), who was about ten years old, and gave him instructions that when he became twenty-four years old or so, he should go to the land Antum and retrieve the plates of Nephi from a hill called Shim, which was near the city of Jershon, where Ammaron had buried the sacred writings. He instructed Mormon[2] to record all he observed among the people onto the plates of Nephi.

12

People First Mentioned in the Book of Mormon

Note: **Mormon²** (#159) and his son, **Moroni²** (#162), are first mentioned in the Words of Mormon, not in the Book of Mormon. However, they were mentioned out of sequence, long before their actual births. They were briefly referred to at that time. Their narratives follow now in the appropriate chronological sequence.

159.* MORMON²

Words of Mormon 1:1. <u>MORMON²</u>, son of **Mormon¹** (#160), abridged the plates containing the record of king **Benjamin** (#30). He interjected commentary from time to time throughout his abridgment. As a result, when we first learn of him in The Words of Mormon, he is out of chronological order by about 450 years. [The Words of Mormon are inserted between The Book of Omni which ends 130 B.C. and The Book of Mosiah which begins 130 B.C.]

Helaman 12. Mormon² editorialized regarding the foolishness and nothingness of man compared to the power of God, and stated that in the day of judgment, men shall have everlasting life or everlasting damnation, depending on whether they have done good or evil during this life.

3 Nephi 5. Mormon² said he made his record according to the record of **Nephi¹** (#6), which was engraven on plates called the plates of Nephi. He said that there are many records, but that this book cannot contain a hundredth of the things that actually transpired. He made his record on plates which he made with his own hands.

He is called Mormon after the land of Mormon in which **Alma¹** (#45) established the church. He is a disciple of **Jesus Christ** (#143). "I have been called of him to declare his word among his people, that they might have everlasting life" [v. 13]. He said that the time will come when the seed of **Jacob**[1] (SA #8) will be gathered together unto their own lands from the four quarters of the world. He is a pure descendant of **Lehi**[1] (#1).

Mormon 1:1. He was born about A.D. 311. When Mormon[2] was about 10 years old, **Ammaron** (#158) went to him and told him that he perceived that he was a sober child and quick to observe. He told him to remember the things he observed happening among the people, and that when he reached the age of twenty-four years he should go to the land Antum, unto a hill called Shim, and recover the sacred records which Ammaron had buried there. He was told to only take the plates of Nephi and to leave the rest hidden in the hill. Ammaron instructed him that he was to record the things that he observed concerning this people.

Mormon[2] told us that his father was also named Mormon[1] and that he is a descendant of Nephi[1] (#6).

When he was 11 years old, his family moved southward to Zarahemla. War between the **Nephites** (#13) and the **Lamanites** (#12) surrounded the borders of Zarahemla. As many as 30,000 men were in the Nephite army. The Nephites were temporarily victorious, and there was peace for about four years. Because of wickedness, the Lord ceased the work of miracles: no gifts came from the Lord, and the Holy Ghost did not come upon any.

When Mormon[2] was 15 years old, he was visited of the Lord. He attempted to preach, but was forbidden to do so because the people had willfully rebelled. The **Gadianton robbers** (#126) infested the whole land and so people began to hide up their treasures, but they "became slippery" [v. 18].

Mormon 2. When Mormon[2] was in his 16th year, he was appointed by the people to be the leader of their armies. [326 years had now passed away since the birth of the Savior.] The Lamanite king, **Aaron**[4] (#161), came against Mormon[2] with an army of 44,000 people. Mormon[2] defeated him with his army of 42,000. [Three hundred and thirty years had now passed away.] The Nephites began to repent of their iniquity, but their sorrowing was not unto repentance but, rather, "the sorrowing of the damned because the Lord would not always suffer them to take happiness in sin" [v. 13].

Wars continued for the next several years. In the 346th year, the Lamanites came with an army of 50,000. The Nephite army numbered 30,000. The Nephites were victorious, but the Lord was not with them. In the 350th year, they made a treaty with the Lamanites and the robbers of Gadianton wherein the land was divided and the Nephites got the land northward, the Lamanites the land southward.

Mormon 3. From the 350th year through the 360th year, there was peace. In the 361st and 362nd years, the Lamanites came to battle. The Nephites were victorious, but swore they would avenge the deaths of their people by going up against the Lamanites. Mormon², now about 51 years old, refused to be their leader from this time on and stood as an idle witness to the events that transpired and recorded them, as commanded by the Lord.

Mormon² reiterated that his people will be judged by the twelve disciples whom Jesus called in this land [America]. They, in turn, will be judged by the twelve apostles chosen in Jerusalem. We must all stand to be judged of our works. He wished he could persuade all people to repent and prepare to stand before the judgment-seat of Christ.

Mormon 4. Because the Nephites went up unto the Lamanites contrary to the Lord's will, they were defeated. "It is by the wicked that the wicked are punished," he said [v. 5]. The Nephites repulsed the Lamanites in the 364th year. In the 366th year, there were still more battles. Thousands had been slain on both sides. The Lamanites were sacrificing the Nephite women and children up unto their idol gods. In angry retaliation, the Nephites drove them out of their lands. The Lamanites did not come against them again until A.D. 375. From this point on, the Nephites never gained power over the Lamanites, but began to be swept off the earth by them.

Mormon² gathered up all the sacred records from the hill Shim to protect them.

Mormon 5. Mormon² repented of the oath he had made to never lead the Nephite armies again and agreed to be their leader, but he was without hope because of their wickedness. By A.D. 380, the carnage was so great that Mormon[2] dared not give a full account; thus, he abridged what was happening. The record was being written unto the remnant of the house of Jacob[1] (SA #), to come forth according to the Lord's own due time and in his own way, for the purpose of persuading the Jews that Jesus is the Christ. The Lamanites would be scattered by the Gentiles "who shall possess the land" [v. 19] and would become a dark, a filthy, and a loathsome people. He again urged them to repent.

Mormon 6. Mormon[2] wrote an epistle to the king of the Lamanites requesting that they gather all their people together unto the land of Cumorah, by a hill called Cumorah, for one last battle. In A.D. 385, they had now all gathered together at the designated place. Mormon[2] hid up the sacred records, all except a few plates which he gave unto his son, **Moroni**[2] (#162). The battle that ensued saw the final destruction of the Nephites: 230,000 were slain; only 24 Nephites survived, "and also a few who had escaped into the south countries, and a few who had deserted over unto the Lamanites" [v. 15]. Mormon[2] was wounded, but not killed, in this battle.

Mormon 7. Mormon[2] concluded his record by speaking to the remnant of the house of Israel, inviting them to believe in Christ, indicating that there are two sets of records that testify of Christ. He said, "Therefore repent, and be baptized in the name of Jesus, and lay hold upon the gospel of Christ, which shall be set before you, not only in this record [The Book of Mormon] but also in the record which shall come unto the Gentiles from the Jews [the Bible], which record shall come from the Gentiles unto you. For behold, this [The Book of Mormon] is written for the intent that ye may believe that [the Bible]; and if ye believe that [the Bible] ye will believe this [The Book of Mormon] also; and if ye believe this [The Book of Mormon] ye will know concerning your fathers, and also the marvelous works which were wrought by the power of God among them" [vs. 8-9]. Mormon's[2] son, Moroni[2], the last Nephite survivor, finished the record, beginning with Mormon 8.

160. MORMON[1]

Mormon 1:5. **MORMON**[1], the father of **Mormon**[2] (#159), carried him "into the land southward, even to the land of Zarahemla" when Mormon[2] was eleven years old.

161. AARON[4]

Mormon 2:9. **AARON**[4] was king of the **Lamanites** (#12) around A.D. 330. [**Aaron**[1] (SB #1) was the brother of **Moses** (SA #2). **Aaron**[2] (#219) was a Jaredite king. **Aaron**[3] (#52) was the son of **Mosiah**[2] (#32).]

In A.D. 361, Aaron[4] sent an epistle to **Mormon**[2] (#159) indicating he and his warriors were coming against them in battle. He came against the **Nephites** (#13) with an army of 44,000 people. Mormon[2] withstood him with an army of 42,000.

Moroni 9:17. Mormon[2], in his epistle to **Moroni**[2] (#162), reported that those Nephites who fled to the army of Aaron[4] fell victims to their awful brutality, which at this time even included cannibalism.

162.* MORONI[2]

Words of Mormon 1:1. **MORONI**[2] is first referred to in The Words of Mormon which **Mormon**[2] (#159) inserted earlier in The Book of Mormon at a point of time about 130 B.C. In The Words of Mormon, Mormon[2] had just completed his abridgment of the records and was preparing to turn the plates over to his son, Moroni [A.D. 385]. [**Moroni**[1] (#97) was a Nephite military commander who lived between 100 B.C. and 56 B.C.]

Mormon 6:6. Moroni[2] was the son of Mormon[2]. He was a military leader and one of the 24 people to survive the final battle at the hill Cumorah. Somewhere around A.D. 385, Mormon[2] turned the record keeping over to him.

Mormon 8. Moroni's[2] record begins in A.D. 401. Many years had passed since the battle of Cumorah in A.D. 385. By the time Moroni[2] began his record, all the **Nephites** (#13) had been slain except Moroni[2]. Moroni[2] was totally alone. The three Nephite disciples had tarried among the Nephites until the people became too wicked. Although Mormon² and Moroni² had seen them, Moroni² indicated that no man knows whether or not they are still upon the face of the land [v. 10].

Moroni² testified that the record [The Book of Mormon] would come forth by the power of God and by none other. Those who work against the Lord shall be in danger of being hewn down and cast into the fire. The Lord's purposes will continue till all his promises shall be fulfilled. The Book of Mormon would come forth in a day of wickedness: fires, tempests, and vapors of smoke in foreign lands; wars, rumors of wars, and earthquakes in divers places; great pollutions would be upon the face of the land: murders, robbing, lying, deceiving, whoredoms, and all manner of abominations.

Mormon 9. Moroni² calls upon the unbelievers to repent and come unto **Christ** (#143). He reminds us that God is a God of miracles: God is the same yesterday, today, and forever! Miracles cease only because of the unbelief of man. He reminds us of the fall of **Adam** (SA #4) and the plan of redemption. He also teaches that signs shall follow those that believe: in Christ's name they shall cast out devils, speak with new tongues, take up serpents, avoid the effects of poison, heal the sick. He urges those who receive his record to seek to serve God and remain faithful, enduring to the end.

Ether 4. Moroni² was commanded by the Lord to seal up the writings of the **brother of Jared²** (#181.) The Lord told him that those writings shall not be revealed until men have faith even as the brother of Jared². Christ commanded men to believe his words and those of his disciples. In the book of Ether, the Lord calls people to repent and come unto him, to believe in his gospel and be baptized in his name that they might be saved. Signs shall follow those who believe in his name.

Ether 5. Moroni² stressed that in the Lord's due time, three witnesses would be shown the plates; the testimony of these three witnesses and the book itself would stand as a testimony against the world at the last day, and shall stand as a testimony of the truthfulness of The Book of Mormon. [*Note:* In the Introduction to The Book of Mormon, Oliver

Cowdery, David Whitmer, and Martin Harris, testify "That we, through the grace of God the Father, and our Lord Jesus Christ, have seen the plates which contain this record . . . ."]

Moroni 1. Moroni[2] abridged the record of the Jaredites which is contained in the Book of Ether. [See 179 through 238]. Between A.D. 400 and A.D. 421, inasmuch as he was still alive, he decided to record a few more thoughts.

Moroni 2. Moroni[2] indicated that Christ had given his disciples power to bestow the Holy Ghost and had told them the manner in which it should be done.

Moroni 3. Moroni[2] explained how priests and teachers were called and ordained by the elders.

Moroni 4. He explained how the elders and priests administered the sacramental bread.

Moroni 5. He explained the mode of administering the sacramental wine.

Moroni 6. Moroni[2] explained who should be baptized, removal of names from the records, about reinstating them "as oft as they repented," and recorded that members of the church met often. Meetings were conducted according to the Spirit.

Moroni 7. Moroni[2] recorded some of his father's words regarding faith, hope and charity. Mormon[2] had counseled that a person will be judged by his fruits, and that if a man offereth a gift or prayeth without real intent, it profiteth him nothing. An evil man cannot do that which is good. That which is good cometh of God; that which is evil cometh from the devil. Every man is given the Spirit of Christ that he may know good from evil. "It is by faith that miracles are wrought . . . wherefore, if these things have ceased wo be unto the children of men, for it is because of unbelief, and all is vain" [v. 37]. "If a man have faith he must needs have hope . . . through the atonement of Christ and the power of his resurrection, to be raised unto life eternal . . . for without faith there cannot be any hope" [vs. 41-42]. If ye have not charity, ye are nothing, for charity never faileth. Charity is the pure love of Christ and is the greatest of all the gifts of God [vs. 46-47].

Moroni 8. Moroni² recorded more words of his father, Mormon², which Mormon² had written to him shortly after Moroni² had been called to the ministry years earlier. Mormon² counseled that infant baptism is an evil abomination before God. Little children are not capable of committing sin. Moroni² was instructed to teach repentance and baptism unto those who were accountable and capable of committing sin.

Moroni 9. Moroni² recorded a second epistle he had received from his father wherein Mormon² recounted some of the losses they had incurred in battle and painted a picture of the depravity of both the Nephites and the **Lamanites** (#12). **Archeantus** (#174), **Luram** (#175) and **Emron** (#176) had fallen in battle, along with a great number of their choice men.

In this epistle, Mormon² told Moroni² that **Amoron** (#177) had reported to him that the Lamanites had taken many Nephites prisoner from the tower of Sherrizah: the Lamanites had slain the men, and the women and children were fed the flesh of their husbands and fathers. Meanwhile, the Nephites in Moriantum were equally or even more wicked: they robbed their female Lamanite prisoners of chastity, tortured and murdered them, and then devoured their flesh. The Nephite military leader **Zenephi** (#178) had taken the provisions belonging to the widows and daughters who remained in Sherrizah, leaving them to wander whithersoever they could in search of food. Many of the widows and daughters were perishing for want of food. Those Nephites who fled to the army of king **Aaron⁴** (#161) had fallen victim to the awful brutality of the Lamanites. [This epistle was written to Moroni² prior to the time his father delivered the sacred records to him.]

Moroni 10. Moroni², in this, the final chapter of The Book of Mormon, bore his testimony to the future Lamanites. More than 420 years had passed since the sign was given of the coming of Christ [c. A.D. 421]. Moroni² was preparing to seal up the record. He stressed that a testimony of the truthfulness of the things written in this book [The Book of Mormon] comes by the power of the Holy Ghost to those who ask God, in the name of Christ, with a sincere heart, with real intent, having faith in Christ. God works by power, according to the faith of the children of men. There are many gifts of God, and there are different ways that these gifts are administered, but they are given by the Holy Ghost unto men to profit them. Every good gift comes of Christ. These gifts will exist to the end of the world, as long as people are faithful.

THE NEPHITE MILITARY LEADERS WHO FELL WITH THEIR 10,000 EACH IN THE FINAL BATTLE

163. GIDGIDDONAH

Mormon 6:13. **GIDGIDDONAH** was a Nephite commander [c. A.D. 385] who fell with his 10,000 at the final battle.

164. LAMAH

Mormon 6:14. **LAMAH** was a Nephite commander [c. A.D. 385] who fell with his 10,000 at the final battle.

165. GILGAL

Mormon 6:14. **GILGAL** was a Nephite commander [c. A.D. 385] who fell with his 10,000 at the final battle.

166. LIMHAH

Mormon 6:14. **LIMHAH** was a Nephite commander [c. A.D. 385] who fell with his 10,000 at the final battle.

167. JENEUM

Mormon 6:14. **JENEUM** was a Nephite commander [c. A.D. 385] who fell with his 10,000 at the final battle.

168. CUMENIHAH

Mormon 6:14. <u>CUMENIHAH</u> was a Nephite commander [c. A.D. 385] who fell with his 10,000 at the final battle.

169. MORONIHAH[2]

Mormon 6:14. <u>MORONIHAH</u>[2] was a Nephite commander [c. A.D. 385] who fell with his 10,000 at the final battle. [**Moronihah**[1] (#116) was the son of Moroni[1] (#97).]

170. ANTIONUM

Mormon 6:14. ANTIONUM was a Nephite commander [c. A.D. 385] who fell with his 10,000 at the final battle.

171. SHIBLOM[2]

Mormon 6:14. <u>SHIBLOM</u>[2] was a Nephite commander [c. A.D. 385] who fell with his 10,000 at the final battle. [**Shiblom**[1] (#224) was a late Jaredite king.]

172. SHEM[2]

Mormon 6:14. <u>SHEM</u>[2] was a Nephite commander [c. A.D. 385] who fell with his 10,000 at the final battle. [**Shem**[1] (SB #2) was the son of Noah[1] (SA #26).]

173. JOSH

Mormon 6:14. <u>JOSH</u> was a Nephite commander [c. A.D. 385] who fell with his 10,000 at the final battle.

Note: There were also an additional 10 unnamed leaders, each with their 10,000, who fell.

174. ARCHEANTUS

Moroni 9:2. <u>ARCHEANTUS</u> was apparently a Nephite military officer. **Mormon**[2] (#159) wrote his son **Moroni**[2] (#162) an epistle indicating that Archeantus had fallen in battle along with **Luram** (#175) and **Emron** (#176).

175. LURAM

Moroni 9:2. <u>LURAM</u> was apparently a Nephite military officer. **Mormon**[2] (#159) wrote his son **Moroni**[2] (#162) an epistle indicating that Luram had fallen in battle along with **Archeantus** (#174) and **Emron** (#176).

176. EMRON

Moroni 9:2. <u>EMRON</u> was apparently a Nephite military officer. **Mormon**[2] (#159) wrote his son **Moroni**[2] (#166) an epistle indicating that Emron had fallen in battle along with **Archeantus** (#174) and **Luram** (#175).

177. AMORON

Moroni 9:7. <u>AMORON</u> was apparently a Nephite who carried a report to **Mormon**[2] (#159). Mormon[2] indicated in his epistle to **Moroni**[2] (#162) that Amoron had reported that the **Lamanites** (#12) had taken many **Nephites** (#13) prisoner from the tower of Sherrizah: the Lamanites had slain the men, and the women and children were given very little water and were fed the flesh of their husbands and fathers.

178. ZENEPHI

Moroni 9:16. <u>ZENEPHI</u> was a Nephite military officer who carried off the provisions of the widows and the daughters, leaving them to wander wherever they could in search of food, resulting in the deaths of many of the older widows.

13

People First Mentioned in the Book of Ether

THE RECORD OF THE PEOPLE OF JARED²

The record of the Jaredites was taken from the twenty-four plates found by the people of Limhi (#39) in the days of king Mosiah² (#32) and was abridged by Moroni² (#162). Following the narratives on each of the Jaredites, there is a chart that shows the lineage of the Jaredites which can aid in following the intrigue as family members contend for power.

179. JAREDITES

Heading. The **JAREDITES** were the descendants of **Jared²** (#180), the brother of **Jared²** (#181), and their friends whose language was not confounded by the Lord at the tower of Babel.

Ether 2. After petitioning the Lord, these people were guided away from Babel, across the waters, to America. They traveled across the waters in eight barges built according to the Lord's instructions.

Ether 6. The barges were driven by the winds to the land of promise. They carried animals and provisions for both people and animals. They were on the water 344 days. They humbled themselves and shed tears of joy when they reached land. They were taught to walk humbly before the Lord. They multiplied greatly and spread out over the land.

When Jared² and his brother were getting old, they gathered the people together to inquire as to their wishes. The people desired one of their sons to be king over them. None of the sons of the brother of Jared² would be king. Finally, **Orihah** (#185), one of the sons of Jared², agreed to be king.

Ether 7. Orihah reigned righteously but, eventually over the years and as succeeding kings reigned, rival kingdoms of **Shule** (#189) and **Cohor**² (#192), Shule's nephew's son, split the kingdom. Prophets condemned the wickedness of the people, but the people mocked them. Nevertheless, king Shule supported the prophets.

Ether 8. Under **Akish** (#199), a wicked band of people with secret oaths and covenants was formed.

Ether 9. The reigns of government were passed from one person to another through descent, intrigue and murder. A famine and poisonous serpents plagued the people. War saw the destruction of all but 30 of Akish's people and a few who fled to the house of **Omer** (#194).

Ether 10. The reigns of government continued to pass from one person to another. Some kings ruled in righteousness, others in wickedness. When the people were righteous, they prospered and were blessed by the Lord. More often than not, the people were wicked.

Ether 11. Their lives were dominated by wickedness, strife and war. The people rejected the prophets, and the prophets prophesied of their eventual destruction.

Ether 14. The wickedness of the people resulted in blood and carnage throughout all the land. The final battle saw the total destruction of the Jaredites with only **Coriantumr**² (#232) and the prophet **Ether** (#231) left alive to witness it, as prophesied by Ether.

Omni 1:21. Coriantumr², the last of the Jaredites, was discovered by the people of **Zarahemla** (#28). He dwelt with them for the space of nine moons. The people of Zarahemla carried the records of Coriantumr² and his people to **Mosiah**² (#32), who interpreted them by the gift and power of God.

180. JARED²

Ether 1:33. <u>JARED</u>² was the founder of the **Jaredites** (#179). One of his four sons was **Orihah** (#185). [**Jared**¹ (SB #3) was the father of

Enoch[2] (Old Testament), neither of whom are mentioned in The Book of Mormon.] Jared's[2] story begins at the time of the confounding of the languages at the tower of Babel. Jared[2] asked his **brother** (#181) to petition the Lord that their language might not be confounded. He had him petition the Lord a second time so that the language of their friends might not be confounded. Again he asked him to petition the Lord to inquire as to where the Lord might have them go.

Ether 6. Jared[2] had four sons and eight daughters. When the people wanted Jared[2] and his brother to provide them with a king, the brother of Jared[2] was reluctant, but Jared[2] told him to suffer them to have one. When none of the sons of the brother of Jared[2] would agree to be king, they wanted one of Jared's[2] sons to be king. The older three all refused. Finally, **Orihah** (#185) agreed to become king. Both Jared[2] and his brother died.

181. JARED'S[2] BROTHER

Ether 1:33. THE BROTHER OF JARED[2] was a large and mighty man, highly favored of the Lord. His brother **Jared**[2] (#180) asked him to petition the Lord that their language might not be confounded. He did so, and the Lord did not confound their languages nor that of their friends and their families. The brother of Jared[2] prayed a third time and inquired as to where the Lord would send them. The Lord told them he would lead them to a new land, choice above all others, and for them to gather together their flocks and seeds of every kind, etc.

[*Note:* In an article in **BOOK OF MORMON** (Religion 121-122) Student Manual, copyright 1981, Corporation of the President, Church of Jesus Christ of Latter-day Saints, p. 478, Mr. George Reynolds relates a story first published in *The Juvenile Instructor*, May 1, 1892, "The Jaredites," p. 282, wherein the prophet Joseph Smith indicated that the brother of Jared's[2] name was Mahonri Moriancumer.]

Ether 2. The Lord brought them to "that great sea which divideth the land" [v. 13]. They pitched their tents and lived there four years. They called the place Moriancumer. After four years, the Lord again talked to the brother of Jared[2] and chastised him for not calling upon him. The brother of Jared² repented and then called upon the Lord in behalf of his brethren. The Lord instructed them to build barges "after the manner of barges which ye have hitherto built" [v. 16]. They were tight like unto a dish, and the length was that of a tree. But there were no windows for air or light. The brother of Jared² inquired of the Lord how they could breathe and how they could see. The Lord told him to make a hole in the top and bottom of each boat that could be unstopped to give them air. When the brother of Jared² complained about the lack of light, the Lord instructed him to come up with a solution. "What will ye that I should do that ye may have light in your vessels?" [v. 23].

Ether 3. These people had built eight barges. The brother of Jared² went unto a mount and moltened out of rock 16 small stones which were like transparent glass. Then he prayed unto the Lord and asked him to touch the stones with his finger and make them shine forth. The Lord did so, and the brother of Jared² saw the finger of the Lord. In fear, he fell to the earth because he did not know the Lord had a body like unto flesh and blood. Because the brother of Jared² had such great faith, the Lord showed his whole body of spirit to him and ministered unto him, even as he ministered unto the Nephites [v. 18]. The Lord showed the brother of Jared² all the inhabitants of the earth which had been and all that there would be unto the ends of the earth. The Lord commanded him to not make these things known but to seal them up, along with two stones which would magnify to the eyes of men the things which the brother of Jared² was commanded to write, to come forth in the Lord's own due time.

Ether 4-5. The brother of Jared² was commanded to write the things he saw, but they were forbidden to come forth until after **Jesus** (#143) was lifted up upon the cross. Thus, king **Mosiah**² (#32) kept them and did not show them unto the people. Later, because of the wickedness of the people, **Moroni**² (#162) was also commanded to seal them up.

Ether 6. The brother of Jared² put one stone in each end of the eight barges; thus, they had light for the 344 days they were driven upon the waters by winds that "never did cease to blow towards the promised land" [v. 8]. When they reached the shore, they bowed themselves down upon the land, humbled themselves, and shed tears of joy before the Lord because of his tender mercies.

The brother of Jared[2] had twenty-two sons and daughters. When the people requested that they be given a king, the brother of Jared[2] prophesied that it would lead them into captivity. Nevertheless, he complied with Jared's[2] request to give them what they wanted. The people wanted **Pagag** (#186), the son of the brother of Jared[2], to be king. He and all of his brothers refused to be king. Finally, one of the sons of Jared[2], **Orihah** (#185), agreed to be king. Jared[2] and his brother died.

182. JACOM

Ether 6:14. <u>JACOM</u> was one of the four sons of **Jared**[2] (#180). He refused to be king.

183. GILGAH

Ether 6:14. <u>GILGAH</u> was one of the four sons of **Jared**[2] (#180). He refused to be king.

184. MAHAH

Ether 6:14. <u>MAHAH</u> was one of the four sons of **Jared**[2] (#180). He refused to be king.

185. ORIHAH

Ether 6:14. <u>ORIHAH</u> was one of the four sons of **Jared**[2] (#180). After all of the sons of the **brother of Jared**[2] (#181) refused to be king, and after his three older brothers refused to be king, he finally agreed to become king when the people insisted upon having one.

Ether 7. Orihah lived many days and reigned in righteousness all his days. He had thirty-one children: eight daughters and twenty-three sons. In his later years, he begat **Kib** (#187), and Kib reigned in his stead.

186. PAGAG

Ether 6:25. <u>PAGAG</u> was the eldest son of the **brother of Jared**[2] (#181). When the people chose him to be king, he refused. The people wanted the brother of Jared[2] to constrain him to be their king, but the brother of Jared[2] said no man should ever be constrained to be king. All of Pagag's brothers also refused to become king. Finally, **Jared's**[2] (#180) youngest son, **Orihah** (#185), agreed to be their king.

187. KIB

Ether 7:3. <u>KIB</u> was the son of **Orihah** (#185), begotten in Orihah's old age. He succeeded his father as king. He begat **Corihor**[1] (#188). When Corihor[1] was 32 years old, he rebelled against his father, raised an army and took him captive. Kib and his people dwelled in captivity until he was exceedingly old. In his old age, while in captivity, Kib begat **Shule** (#189). Shule eventually raised an army, went against his brother Corihor[1] and restored the kingdom to his father. Kib, in turn, bestowed the kingdom on Shule.

188. CORIHOR[1]

Ether 7:3. <u>CORIHOR</u>[1] was the son of **Kib** (#187); the grandson of **Orihah** (#185); and also the great-grandson of **Jared**[2] (#180). [**Corihor**[2] (#234) was a late Jaredite.] When Corihor[1] was thirty- two years old, he rebelled against his father. He gathered together an army and took his father captive. His brother **Shule** (#189), who was born in captivity in his father's old age, went against Corihor[1] in battle, and restored the kingdom to their father. Therefore, Kib conferred the kingdom on Shule. Corihor[1] repented and was given power in the kingdom. He begat many sons and daughters, among whom was **Noah**[2] (#190).

189. SHULE

Ether 7:7. <u>SHULE </u>was the son of **Kib** (#187) [begotten in Kib's old age]; the grandson of **Orihah** (#185); the great-grandson of **Jared**[2] (#180); and the brother of **Corihor**[1] (#188). Corihor[1] rebelled against his father, Kib, and took him captive. Thus, Shule was born in captivity. He was angry with Corihor[1] and made swords out of steel and formed an army which overthrew Corihor[1]. Shule restored the kingdom to his father. Therefore, Kib bestowed the kingdom on Shule, and Shule began to reign in his father's stead. He had many sons and daughters and reigned in righteousness.

When his brother Corihor¹ repented of his evil ways, Shule gave him power in the kingdom. **Noah²** (#190) and his brother **Cohor¹** (#191), two of Corihor's¹ sons, rebelled against Corihor¹ and Shule, capturing Shule. As they prepared to put him to death, Shule's sons crept into the house and killed Noah². They freed their father and restored him to the kingdom. Upon Noah's² death, his son **Cohor²** (#19) went to battle against Shule but was slain by Shule. Cohor's² son **Nimrod²** (#193) then returned the portion of the kingdom that had been controlled by his father to Shule, gaining favor in the kingdom. When the people began to revile against the prophets, Shule enacted a law which gave the prophets power to go wherever they wanted. The people repented and began to prosper again. He executed judgment in righteousness all of his days.

190. NOAH²

Ether 7:14. **NOAH²,** the son of **Corihor¹** (#188) and father of **Cohor²** (#192), rebelled against both his uncle **Shule** (#189) and against his own father. He drew his brother **Cohor¹** (#191) and all of his brethren and many other people away. He battled Shule and eventually took him captive. As he was about to put Shule to death, Shule's sons crept into the house and killed Noah². They freed their father and restored him to the kingdom. [**Noah¹** (SA #26) was the patriarch at the time of the flood; **Noah³** (#40), son of **Zeniff** (#31), was a wicked king over the Nephites in the land of Nephi.]

191. COHOR¹

Ether 7:15. **COHOR¹,** the son of **Corihor¹** (#188), the brother of **Noah²** (#190) and the uncle of **Cohor²** (#192), followed his brother in rebellion against their uncle **Shule** (#189).

192. COHOR²

Ether 7:20. **COHOR²** was the son of **Noah²** (#190), nephew of **Cohor¹** (#191), and great-nephew of king **Shule** (#189). The kingdom was split into two factions: Cohor's[2] supporters and king Shule's supporters. Shule defeated and killed Cohor[2] in battle. Cohor's[2] son **Nimrod**[2] (#193) returned that portion of the kingdom to Shule.

193. NIMROD[2]

Ether 7:22. **NIMROD**[2] was the son of **Cohor**[2] (#192). Upon Cohor's[2] death, Nimrod[2] gave the kingdom back to **Shule** (#189), his great-great-uncle. He gained favor in the kingdom and could do according to his desires. [**Nimrod**[1] (SA #34) was the grandson of Ham in the Old Testament. The valley of Nimrod mentioned in Ether 2:1 was named after this mighty hunter.]

194. OMER

Ether 8:1. **OMER** was the son of **Shule** (#189) and reigned in the stead of Shule. He begat **Jared**[3] (#195). Jared[3] rebelled against Omer, drawing away half of the kingdom. Omer was taken captive by Jared[3]. He was in captivity half of his life. He also begat other sons and daughters, among whom was **Esrom** (#196) and **Coriantumr**[1] (#197). They rose up against their brother Jared[3] and restored the kingdom to Omer.

Ether 9. When Jared[3] promised **Akish** (#199) his daughter's hand in return for Omer's head, the Lord warned Omer in a dream to depart out of the land with his family. All of Omer's family left, with the exception of Jared[3], who was then anointed king over the people. Akish, Jared's[3] son-in-law, wanted to be king and had Jared[3] murdered, and then he ruled. Akish starved one of his **own sons** (#201) to death out of jealousy, so another son, **Nimrah** (#202), and a small band fled unto Omer. Akish's other sons went to war against their father for many years. This resulted in almost the total destruction of the people: only 30 survived among those who had not fled unto Omer. Thus, the kingdom was restored again to Omer. He begat **Emer** (#203) in his old age, and Emer was anointed to reign in his stead. Omer lived two more years, during which time there was peace.

195. JARED³

Ether 8:1. <u>JARED</u>³ was the evil son of **Omer** (#194). [**Jared**¹ (SB #3) is the father of Enoch² in the Old Testament. No mention is made of either of them in The Book of Mormon. **Jared**² (#180) was the founder of the Jaredites. He and his brother brought their people to America at the time of the confounding of the languages.] Jared³ rebelled against his father, led half the kingdom away, and took his father captive. His brothers **Esrom** (#196) and **Coriantumr**¹ (#197) rose up against Jared³ and defeated his army. He pleaded for his life so his brothers did not slay him. **Jared's**³ **daughter** (#198) saw her father's sorrow at losing the kingdom and the power he desired. She put into his heart a plan whereby he could get the kingdom by killing his father. However, Omer was warned in a dream to flee with his family. Jared³ was then anointed king over the people. He gave his daughter in marriage to **Akish** (#199), who had agreed to kill Omer. Akish, however, decided he wanted the kingdom himself, and he had Jared³ murdered while he sat upon the throne. Akish then became king.

196. ESROM

Ether 8:4. <u>ESROM</u> was one of **Omer's** (#194) sons and a brother of **Jared**³ (#195). He and his brother **Coriantumr**¹ (#197) defeated Jared's³ army in battle. They spared Jared's³ life and returned the kingdom to their father, Omer.

197. CORIANTUMR¹

Ether 8:4. <u>CORIANTUMR</u>¹ was one of **Omer's** (#194) sons and a brother of **Jared**³ (#195). He and his brother **Esrom** (#196) defeated Jared's³ army in battle, but they spared Jared's³ life. They returned the kingdom to their father, Omer. [**Coriantumr**² (#232) was the final king of the Jaredites. **Coriantumr**³ (#123) was a Nephite dissenter.]

198. JARED'S³ DAUGHTER

Ether 8:8. <u>JARED'S</u>³ <u>DAUGHTER</u> is not mentioned by name. However, she was very wicked. When she saw how sorry her father was at losing the kingdom when his brothers defeated him in battle, she suggested a plan whereby he could regain the kingdom. She put it into her father's heart to kill her grandfather **Omer** (#194) by having her dance before **Akish** (#199), a friend of Omer's. When Akish desired to have her for a wife, Jared³ was to tell him that he could marry her if he would bring Omer's head to him.

199. AKISH

Ether 8:10. <u>AKISH</u> was the son of **Kimnor** (#200). He desired to marry **Jared's³ daughter** (#198). She was promised to him on condition that he bring king **Omer's** (#194) head to **Jared³** (#195). He established secret combinations and plotted with his kindred and friends to accomplish this deed. Omer had been a friend to Akish, who now plotted to take his life.

Ether 9. Omer was warned in a dream to flee with his family so Akish did not get to kill him. Nevertheless, Jared³ gave his daughter to Akish for a wife. Akish decided he wanted the kingdom for himself and had Jared³ killed while he sat upon the throne. Therefore, he became king. He became jealous of one of **his own sons** (#201) and imprisoned him and starved him to death. This angered another son, **Nimrah** (#202), who gathered together a small band. They fled unto his great-grandfather Omer. Akish's remaining sons won the hearts of the people. There were wars between Akish and his sons which lasted for many years, resulting in the destruction of nearly all of the kingdom. Only 30 people survived in addition to those who had fled unto Omer. Thus, the kingdom was restored unto Omer.

200. KIMNOR

Ether 8:10. <u>KIMNOR</u> was the father of **Akish** (#199).

201. SON OF AKISH

Ether 9:7. This <u>SON OF AKISH</u> was imprisoned and starved to death by his father because **Akish** (#199) became jealous of him.

202. NIMRAH

Ether 9:9. <u>NIMRAH</u> was a son of **Akish** (#199). When his father imprisoned **his brother** (#201) and starved him to death, Nimrah gathered a small band together and fled unto his great-grandfather **Omer** (#194), the exiled king.

203. EMER

Ether 9:14. <u>EMER</u> was the son of **Omer** (#194). He was begotten in Omer's old age. Emer was anointed king to reign in Omer's stead. Omer died two years later. Emer executed judgment in righteousness all of his days. The people prospered greatly in the space of sixty-two years. Emer begat many sons and daughters, among whom was **Coriantum**[1] (#204), whom he anointed to reign in his stead, after which he lived four more years. He saw the **Son of Righteousness** (#143).

204. CORIANTUM[1]

Ether 9:21. CORIANTUM[1] was the son of **Emer** (#203) and grandson of **Omer** (#194). [**Coriantum**[2] (#221) was a middle Jaredite who lived in captivity his entire life.] Coriantum[1] was anointed king after Emer. He walked in the steps of his father and reigned righteously. He was a great builder. He had no children until he was very old. His wife died at 102 years of age. He then married a young maid and had sons and daughters. He lived to be 142 years old. He begat **Com**[1] (#205), who reigned in his stead.

205. COM[1]

Ether 9:25. <u>COM</u>[1] was the son of **Coriantum**[1] (#204). [**Com**[2] (#222), a later Jaredite king, was blessed because he protected the prophets.] Com[1] reigned 49 years and begat **Heth**[1] (#206). He also had other sons and daughters. Heth[1] rebelled against his father and embraced the secret combinations. He murdered his father with his own sword. Heth[1] reigned in his father's stead.

206. HETH[1]

Ether 9:25. <u>HETH</u>[1] was the son of **Com**[1] (#205). [**Heth**[2] (#218), son of **Hearthrom** (#217), lived his entire life in captivity. *Note:* The superscript numbers are reversed on Heth[1] and Heth[2] in the Index to The Book of Mormon.] Using his own sword, Heth[1] slew his father and then reigned in his stead. He embraced the secret combinations of old, and wickedness became rampant in the land. Prophets came, but were rejected, and some were cast into pits and left to perish. A great dearth came upon the land. There was no rain, and poisonous serpents chased the flocks out of the land but hedged up the way so the people could not flee. Finally, the people repented, but not until Heth[1] and his household [all except **Shez**[1] (#207)] had perished by the famine.

207. SHEZ[1]

Ether 10:1. <u>SHEZ</u>[1] was the father of **Shez**[2] (#208) and a descendant of **Heth**[1] (#206). [Note: In Ether 1:25 where the genealogy is given, it says he was the son of Heth[1]. However, in this verse, it merely says he was a descendant.] Shez[1] remembered the Lord and walked uprightly before him. He begat many sons and daughters, among whom was Shez[2]. Shez[2] rebelled against his father. When Shez[2] was slain by a robber, peace was restored to his father. Shez[1] lived to an exceedingly old age and built up many cities. Another son, **Riplakish** (#209), reigned in his stead.

208. SHEZ[2]

Ether 10:3. <u>SHEZ</u>[2], the eldest son of **Shez**[1] (#207), rebelled against his father. He was slain by a robber because of his exceeding riches.

209. RIPLAKISH

Ether 10:4. <u>RIPLAKISH</u> was another son of **Shez**[1] (#207). He reigned in wickedness after his father died. He had many wives and concubines, placed heavy taxes on the people, and built beautiful, spacious buildings and a beautiful throne for himself. Most of the fine work was done by those who had been cast into prison when they would not or could not pay the heavy taxes. Those who refused to labor were put to death. After

forty-two years of Riplakish's terrible reign, the people rose up against
him, killing him and driving his descendants out of the land.

210. MORIANTON[1]

Ether 10:9. MORIANTON[1] was a descendant of **Riplakish** (#209).
Because Riplakish was such a wicked leader, the people drove him and
his descendants out of the land after enduring forty-two years of his terrible reign. Morianton[1], one of those driven out of the land, raised an
army of outcasts and went back to the city and gave battle to the people.
His army was victorious, and he established himself as king over all the
land. He served the people justly but did not follow the ways of the Lord.
He committed many whoredoms and was cut off from the presence of
the Lord. He lived to an exceedingly great age. He begat **Kim** (#211) and
died eight years after Kim became king. [**Morianton**[2] (#103) was the
founder of a Nephite city about 68 B.C.]

211. KIM

Ether 10:13. KIM was the son of **Morianton**[1] (#210). He did not reign
in righteousness. **Kim's brother** (#212) rose up against him, and Kim
remained in captivity the remainder of his days. He begat many sons and
daughters in captivity, among whom was **Levi**[2] (#213), who served in
captivity for forty-two years after Kim's death.

212. KIM'S BROTHER

Ether 10:14. KIM'S BROTHER was another son of **Morianton**[1]
(#210). He rose up in rebellion against **Kim** (#211) and made him live
in captivity all of his life.

213. LEVI[2]

Ether 10:14. LEVI[2] was the righteous son of **Kim** (#211). [**Levi**[1] (SA
#2) was the son of **Jacob**[1] (SA #8) in the Old Testament and is referred
to in 3 Nephi 24:3.] Levi[2] served in captivity for forty-two years after
the death of his father. He waged war upon his uncle, **Kim's brother**
(#212), the king of the land, and obtained the kingdom. He reigned in

righteousness and the people prospered. He begat sons and daughters, among whom was **Corom** (#214), who reigned after him.

214. COROM

Ether 10:16. <u>COROM</u> was the son of **Levi**[2] (#213) and reigned in righteousness after his father. After living to an old age, his son **Kish** (#215) reigned in his stead.

215. KISH

Ether 10:17. <u>KISH</u> was the son of **Corom** (#214). He reigned as king after his father.

216. LIB[1]

Ether 10:18. **LIB**[1] was the son of **Kish** (#215). [**Lib**[2] (#237) was a late Jaredite king.] Lib[1] reigned righteously. It was in his days that the poisonous serpents were destroyed. Lib[1] became a great hunter. During his reign, the people were very industrious and they bought and sold one with another. They were great craftsmen, working with all kinds of precious metals and materials such as silk and linen. They made all manner of tools and tilled the earth. They also made all kinds of weapons. He lived many years and begat many children, among whom was **Hearthom** (#217).

217. HEARTHOM

Ether 10:29. <u>HEARTHOM</u> was the son of **Lib**[1] (#216). He reigned in the stead of his father. When he had served for twenty-four years, the kingdom was taken away from him, and he served the remainder of his years in captivity. He begat **Heth**[2] (#218) in captivity.

218. HETH[2]

Ether 10:31. <u>HETH</u>[2] was the son of **Hearthom** (#217). [**Heth**[1] (#206) was the son of **Com**[1] (#205).] He was born in captivity and lived in captivity all his days. He begat **Aaron**[2] (#219) in captivity.

219. AARON²

Ether 10:31. <u>AARON</u>² was the son of **Heth**² (#218). [**Aaron**¹ (SB #1) is not referred to in The Book of Mormon but was the brother of Moses (SA #2). **Aaron**³ (#52) was a son of **Mosiah**² (#32).] Aaron² was born in captivity and lived in captivity all his days. He begat **Amnigaddah** (#220).

220. AMNIGADDAH

Ether 10:31. <u>AMNIGADDAH</u> was the son of **Aaron**² (#219). He lived in captivity all his days. He begat **Coriantum**² (#221).

221. CORIANTUM²

Ether 10:31. <u>CORIANTUM</u>² was the son of **Amnigaddah** (#220). He was born in captivity and dwelled in captivity all his life. He begat **Com**² (#222). [**Coriantum**¹ (#204) was the son of **Emer** (#203).]

222. COM²

Ether 10:31. <u>COM</u>², son of **Coriantum**² (#221), was born in captivity. Nevertheless, he drew half the kingdom away and reigned over that half of the kingdom for forty-two years. He fought against king **Amgid** (#223) and obtained the rest of the kingdom. However, robbers adopted the old secret combinations; Com² could not prevail against them. [**Com**¹ (#205) was the son of **Coriantum**¹ (#204).]

Ether 11. Prophets came in Com's² days, but the people would not listen. The prophets fled to Com² for protection. He was blessed of the Lord. He begat sons and daughters, among whom was **Shiblom**¹ (#224), who reigned in his stead.

223. AMGID

Ether 10:32. <u>AMGID</u> was a Jaredite king who was overthrown by **Com**² (#222).

224. SHIBLOM[1]

Ether 11:4. __SHIBLOM__[1] (also spelled __SHIBLON__) was the son of **Com**[2] (#222). [In Ether 1:11-12, where the genealogy is listed, it says, "And Seth was the son of Shiblon. And Shiblon was the son of Com." However, in Ether 11:3-4, it says Com begat Shiblom. The narrative of The Book of Ether uses the spelling with the "m," Shiblom. **Shiblom**[2] (#171) was a Nephite commander about A.D. 385 who fell with his 10,000 men in the final battle.] Following Com[2], Shiblom[1] reigned as king. His **brother** (#225) rose against him in battle. There were terrible wars and great wickedness throughout the land. His brother caused that all the prophets should be put to death. There were famines and pestilences. Finally, the people began to repent, and the Lord began to bless them again. However, Shiblom[1] was eventually slain and his son **Seth**[2] (#226) was brought into captivity.

225. SHIBLOM'S[1] BROTHER

Ether 11:4. __SHIBLOM'S__[1] __BROTHER__, another son of **Com**[2] (#222), is not referred to by name. He rebelled against his brother **Shiblom**[1] (#224) and caused great wars and iniquity to occur. He caused that the prophets should be killed.

226. SETH[2]

Ether 11:9. __SETH__[2] was the son of **Shiblom**[1] (or **Shiblon,** #224). [**Seth**[1] (SB #5) was the son of **Adam** (SA #4).] Seth[2] lived in captivity all of his days. He begat **Ahah** (#227).

227. AHAH

Ether 11:10. __AHAH__ was the son of **Seth**[2] (#226). He gained the kingdom and reigned in wickedness over the people. He caused the shedding of much blood, and his days were few. His son **Ethem** (#228) obtained the kingdom.

228. ETHEM

Ether 11:11. <u>ETHEM</u> was apparently the son of **Ahah** (#227). [*Note:* In Ether 1:9, where the genealogy is listed, it says he was the son of Ahah. However, in Ether 11:11, it merely says he was a descendant of Ahah.] Ethem gained the kingdom and was wicked all his days. Again the prophets came, and again they were rejected. He begat **Moron** (#229).

229. MORON

Ether 11:14. <u>MORON</u> was the son of **Ethem** (#228). He obtained the kingdom and, like his father, ruled in wickedness. A mighty man in wickedness rose up and overthrew half of the kingdom, but Moron eventually overthrew him and regained that half of the kingdom. Another mighty man rose up, a descendant of the **brother of Jared**[2] (#181), and he overthrew Moron. Moron dwelled in captivity the rest of his days. He begat **Coriantor** (#230).

230. CORIANTOR

Ether 11:18. <u>CORIANTOR</u> was the son of **Moron** (#229). He dwelled in captivity all his days. Prophets came again during this time, but the people continued to reject them. He begat **Ether** (#231). Coriantor died in captivity.

231. ETHER

Ether 11:23. <u>ETHER,</u> the son of **Coriantor** (#230), was born in captivity.

Ether 12. **Coriantumr**[2] (#232) was king over all the land during Ether's time. Ether was a prophet of the Lord, and he exhorted the people to believe in God unto repentance lest they should be destroyed. He taught that through faith they could have hope for a better world and a place at the right hand of God.

Ether 13. Ether tried to teach the people many things: he told of how after the waters receded off this land it was a land choice above all others; it was the place of the New Jerusalem. He saw the days of **Christ** (#143).

"And he spake also concerning the house of Israel, and the Jerusalem from whence Lehi should come—after it should be destroyed it should be built up again, a holy city unto the Lord; wherefore, it could not be a new Jerusalem for it had been in a time of old; but it should be built up again, and become a holy city of the Lord; and it should be built unto the house of Israel—And that a New Jerusalem should be built up upon this land, unto the remnant of the seed of Joseph, for which things there had been a type. For as Joseph brought his father down into the land of Egypt, even so he died there; wherefore, the Lord brought a remnant of the seed of Joseph out of the land of Jerusalem, that he might be merciful unto the seed of Joseph that they should perish not, even as he was merciful unto the father of Joseph that he should perish not. Wherefore, the remnant of the house of Joseph shall be built upon this land; and it shall be a land of their inheritance; and they shall build up a holy city unto the Lord, like unto the Jerusalem of old; and they shall no more be confounded, until the end come when the earth shall pass away" [vs. 5-8].

Ether was cast out. He hid in the cavity of a rock by day, and by night he went forth viewing the things which came upon the people. He made his record as he dwelled in the cavity of the rock. During this time, people rose up against the king and there were many wars and much destruction. Ether prophesied that if the king and his household repented, they would be saved; but if not, Coriantumr[2] would see everyone destroyed but himself and would die with the new people who inherited this land.

Ether 15. Ether witnessed the total destruction of Coriantumr[2] and his people. He recorded that the Lord told him to go forth, and he went forth and beheld that all the words of the Lord had been fulfilled. He hid up the record where the people of **Limhi** (#39) eventually found them.

232. CORIANTUMR[2]

Ether 12:1. **CORIANTUMR**[2] was king over all the land during **Ether's** (#231) time. [**Coriantumr**[1] (#197), an earlier **Jaredite** (#179), was one of **Omer's** (#194) sons and a brother of **Jared**[3] (#195); **Coriantumr**[3] (#123) was a Nephite dissenter.]

Ether 13. Ether prophesied unto Coriantumr[2] that if he repented, and all his household, the Lord would give him his kingdom and spare his people; but if not, Coriantumr[2] would live to see everyone destroyed and to see the fulfilling of the prophecies that told of another people receiving the land for their inheritance [see Ether 11:21]. Ether prophesied that Coriantumr[2] would be buried by this other people. Coriantumr[2] would not heed Ether's words.

None of the people would repent. **Shared** (#235) rose up and gave battle to Coriantumr[2], taking him into captivity, but Coriantumr's[2] sons defeated Shared and restored their father to the kingdom. Finally, Coriantumr[2] slew Shared in a battle in the valley of Gilgal.

Ether 14. After Shared was killed, his brother **Gilead** (#236) went to battle against Coriantumr[2]. Gilead was murdered in a secret pass by **Lib**[2] (#237), a member of one of the secret combinations. Then Lib[2] gave battle to Coriantumr[2] and was slain. When Lib[2] was slain by Coriantumr[2], his brother **Shiz** (#238) went to battle in his stead. He went after Coriantumr[2] with a vengeance, burning cities and slaying both women and children. A saying went forth throughout the land, "Who can stand before the army of Shiz? Behold, he sweepeth the earth before him!" [v.18]. The people were divided into the camps of Coriantumr[2] and Shiz. War lasted so long and so many people were killed that the land was covered with the bodies of the dead. A stench filled the air.

Ether 15. Coriantumr[2] and Shiz fought one battle after another over a period of several years. When nearly two million of his people had been slain, Coriantumr[2] wrote an epistle to Shiz requesting a truce. Shiz would not agree to a truce. They eventually gathered all the people [men, women and children] into two camps at the hill Rama, which is the same hill where **Mormon**[2] (#159) hid up the sacred records in his time, and prepared for the final battle. The fighting was fierce and the slaughter was terrible. Coriantumr[2] wrote another epistle to Shiz requesting a truce, but again Shiz would not agree to a truce. After a few days of fighting, there were only fifty-two of Coriantumr's[2] people left and only sixty-nine of Shiz's people. By the next night, only twenty-seven of Coriantumr's[2] people were left and thirty-two of Shiz's people. Finally, there were just the two leaders left, and Coriantumr[2] smote off Shiz's head. Shiz raised up on his hands and then fell, struggled for breath, and then died. Coriantumr[2] fell to the earth as if he had no life. Ether went forth as commanded by the Lord and witnessed the end. Then he hid up the records, which were later discovered by the people of **Limhi** (#39).

Omni 1. Coriantumr[2] was discovered by the people of **Zarahemla** (#28). He dwelled with them for nine moons [v. 21].

233. COHOR[3]

Ether 13:17. <u>COHOR</u>[3] was a late Jaredite. In spite of **Ether's** (#231) prophecies, none of Cohor's[3] children would repent of their sins. [**Cohor**[1] (#191) was the son of **Corihor**[1] (#188). **Cohor**[2] (#192) was the son of **Noah**[2] (#190) and nephew of Cohor[1].]

234. CORIHOR[2]

Ether 13:17. <u>CORIHOR</u>[2] was a late Jaredite. None of his sons or daughters would repent of their sins, in spite of the prophet **Ether's** (#231) prophecies. [**Corihor**[1] (#188) was the son of **Kib** (#187).]

235. SHARED

Ether 13:23. <u>SHARED,</u> a late Jaredite, rose up against **Coriantumr**[2] (#232) and captured him. Later, Shared was defeated by Coriantumr's[2] sons. He was killed in battle with Coriantumr[2] in the valley of Gilgal.

236. GILEAD

Ether 14:3, 8. <u>GILEAD</u> was the brother of **Shared** (#235). He went to battle against **Coriantumr**[2] (#232) and slew part of Coriantumr's[2] army as they were drunken. He then placed himself upon the throne. Before long, however, he was murdered by his high priest.

237. LIB[2]

Ether 14:10. <u>LIB</u>[2] was a late Jaredite king. He was one of the secret combinations. He obtained the kingdom by killing the high priest who killed

Gilead (#236). [**Lib**[1] (#216) was a middle Jaredite king, the son of **Kish** (#215) and the father of **Hearthrom** (#217).] Lib[2] was a man of great stature, "more than any man among the people" [v. 10]. He and **Coriantumr**[2] (#232) battled against each other. When Lib[2] was killed in battle, his brother **Shiz** (#238) came against Coriantumr[2].

238. SHIZ

Ether 14:16, 17. SHIZ was the brother of **Lib**[2] (#237). When Lib[2] was killed in battle by **Coriantumr**[2] (#232), Shiz went to battle in his stead. He went after Coriantumr[2] with a vengeance, burning cities and slaying both women and children. A saying went forth throughout the land, "Who can stand before the army of Shiz? Behold, he sweepeth the earth before him!" [v. 18]. The people were divided into two camps: Coriantumr's[2] and Shiz's. The war lasted so long, and so many people were killed, that the land was covered with the bodies of the dead. A stench filled the air.

Ether 15. Coriantumr[2] and Shiz fought many battles over a period of several years. When nearly two million of his people had been slain, Coriantumr[2] wrote an epistle to Shiz requesting a truce. Shiz would not agree to a truce. They eventually gathered all the people [men, women and children] into two camps at the hill Rama, which is the same hill where **Mormon**[2] (#159) hid up the sacred records in his time, and prepared for the final battle. The fighting was fierce and the slaughter was terrible. Coriantumr[2] wrote another epistle to Shiz requesting a truce, but again Shiz would not agree to a truce. After a few days of fighting, there were only fifty-two of Coriantumr's[2] people left and only sixty-nine of Shiz's people. By the next night, there were only twenty-seven of Coriantumr's[2] people left and thirty-two of Shiz's people. Finally, just Shiz and Coriantumr[2] were left. Shiz had fainted for loss of blood. Coriantumr[2] rested a little while, then he smote off Shiz's head. Shiz raised up on his hands and then fell, struggled for breath, and died. Coriantumr[2] fell to the earth as if he had no life. **Ether** (#231) went forth as commanded by the Lord and witnessed the end. He then hid up the records which were later discovered by the people of **Limhi** (#39).

CHART   179

CHART
THE LINEAGE OF
THE JAREDITES

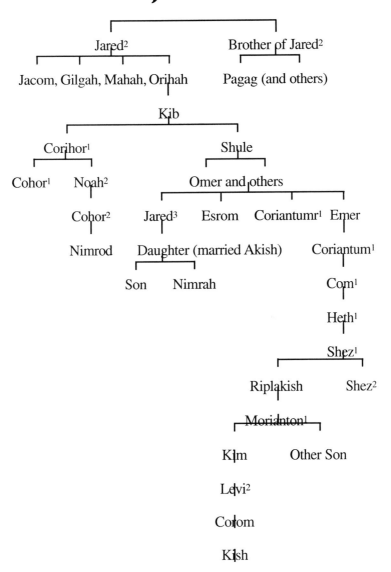

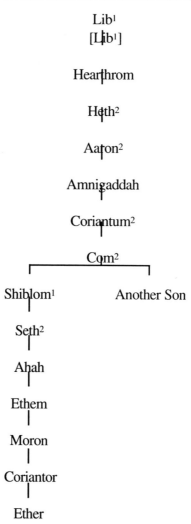

Lib[1]

[Lib[1]]

Hearthrom

Heth[2]

Aaron[2]

Amnigaddah

Coriantum[2]

Com[2]

Shiblom[1]   Another Son

Seth[2]

Ahah

Ethem

Moron

Coriantor

Ether

* The Book of Mormon refers to Morianton[1] only as a descendant of Riplakish, not as a son. Their exact relationship is unknown, as is the number of years between the time Riplakish's descendants were driven out of the land and the time Morianton[1] returned. Ether 10:9 merely says that after the space of many years, Morianton[1], a descendant of Riplakish, returned and gained power over the people.

Addendum

In addition to the foregoing, there are a few other participants in The Book of Mormon who are briefly referred to but are unnamed. They follow in the order they appear in The Book of Mormon.

1. ISHMAEL'S[1] DAUGHTER, SON AND WIFE

1 Nephi 7:19. When **Laman**[1] (#3) and **Lemuel** (#4) sought to lay hands upon **Nephi**[1] (#6) a second time when they were returning to their father's tent in the wilderness with **Ishmael**[1] (#9) and his family, one of **ISHMAEL'S**[1] **DAUGHTERS**, one of his **SONS,** and his **WIFE** pleaded with them in Nephi's[1] behalf, and they let him go.

2. LEHI'S[1] DAUGHTERS

2 Nephi 5:6. Mention is only made in passing that, in addition to his brothers and **Zoram**[1] (#8), **Nephi**[1] (#6) also took his **SISTERS** into the wilderness when **Laman**[1] (#3) and **Lemuel** (#4) sought his life in the promised land. The daughters are never mentioned by name, nor do we know how many there were nor where they fit into the family structure. They were included among those who believed in the warnings and the revelations of God and hearkened unto Nephi's[1] words.

3. AMALEKI'S[1] BROTHER

Omni 1: 30. **AMALEKI'S**[1] **BROTHER** went with **Zeniff** (#31) and his group to try to locate the land of Nephi and **Amaleki**[1] (#26) never heard from him again.

4. LIMHI'S EXPEDITION PARTY CONSISTING OF 43 PEOPLE

Mosiah 8:7. **King Limhi** (#39) was grieved over the plight of his people and sent a party of **43 PEOPLE** out into the wilderness to try to find the land of Zarahemla. Unfortunately, they couldn't find Zarahemla.

However, they did discover a land which was covered with bones of men, and of beasts, and was also covered with ruins of buildings of every kind, having discovered a land which had been peopled with a people who were as numerous as the hosts of Israel [v. 8]. This expedition party returned to King Limhi, carrying with them twenty-four golden plates filled with engravings. [This record is the record of the **Jaredites** (#179).] They also brought breastplates and swords which they found among the ruins.

5. LAMANITE DAUGHTERS

Mosiah 20:1. The **<u>DAUGHTERS OF THE LAMANITES</u>** had a practice of gathering together in a particular place in Shemlon to sing, dance and make merry. One day as they were thus gathered, the **priests of Noah**[3] (#43), who were too ashamed to return to the city of Nephi, carried several of them off into the wilderness.

Mosiah 23. When the Lamanite soldiers who were chasing **Limhi** (#39) and his people accidentally stumbled upon the priests of Noah[3] and the Lamanite daughters who had been abducted, these daughters pleaded for the lives of these men who were now their husbands. The priests joined the Lamanites and were appointed teachers over them. This group of Nephites and apostate Nephite priests discovered **Alma**[1] (#45) and his people in Helam and placed them in bondage.

6. ATTEMPTED SLAYER OF AMMON[2]

Alma 19:22. When **King Lamoni** (#74) and the **queen** (#75) sank to the ground, overcome by the Spirit, the **<u>BROTHER OF ONE OF THE MEN AMMON[2] HAD SLAIN AT THE WATERS OF SEBUS</u>** drew his sword to slay **Ammon**[2], but Ammon[2] could not be slain, and the Lord caused his attacker to fall dead instead.

7. AMALEKITE CONTENDER WITH AARON

Alma 21:5-11. As **Aaron**[3] (#52) preached in Jerusalem, an **<u>AMALEKITE</u>** contended with him, claiming that his people were as good as Aaron's[3], that they believed God would save all men and that they did not believe in the coming of the **Son of God** (#143). They rejected Aaron's[3] words so he left and went to Ani-Anti.

8. SOLDIER OF MORONI[1]

Alma 44:12. When **Moroni**[1] (#97) and **Zerahemnah** (#96) were in a confrontation, Zerahemnah rushed forward to slay Moroni[1]. As he raised his sword, one of **MORONI'S**[1] **SOLDIERS** struck it and broke it. Then he smote Zerahemnah and took his scalp off. He picked the scalp up from off the ground and put it on the point of his sword. Then he warned Zerahemnah's followers, "Even as this scalp has fallen to the earth, which is the scalp of your chief, so shall ye fall to the earth except ye will deliver up your weapons of war and depart with a covenant of peace" [v. 13]. Many threw down their weapons of war and covenanted for peace. Zerahemnah remained angry and stirred the others up to battle. When Zerahemnah saw they were about to be defeated, he cried unto Moroni[1] and promised to covenant for peace. Thus, peace was restored as the eighteenth year of the reign of the judges ended.

9. LAMANITE KING KILLED BY AMALICKIAH'S SERVANTS

Alma 47:1. **Amalickiah** (#99) and his apostate followers, who had fled into the wilderness, joined the Lamanites and stirred them up to anger against the Nephites. The **LAMANITE KING** gave Amalickiah command over that part of the army which was obedient unto the king. They pursued that portion of the army that would not go against the Nephites, which was led by **Lehonti** (#102). Through treachery and deceit, he had Lehonti killed, and then, taking the combined armies back to the Lamanites, Amalickiah had his servants stab the king when he went to raise them up when they bowed to him upon meeting him. Amalickiah then married the queen and gained power over the entire kingdom.

10. SERVANTS OF THE KING OF LAMANITES

Alma 47:25. The **SERVANTS** of the king fled when Amalickiah's servants killed the king and blamed them. They fled to the land of Zarahemla and joined the **people of Ammon**[2] (#84).

Alma 55. **Laman**[4] (#111), who got the Lamanite guards drunk so the Nephites could retake the city of Gid, was one of those servants.

11. AMALICKIAH'S WIFE, THE QUEEN

Alma 47:32. When the **QUEEN** of the Lamanites heard that her husband had been killed [after **Amalickiah** (#99) had cunningly had the king killed by his, Amalickiah's, own servants], she sent for Amalickiah to get a first-hand report. He and the servants testified that the king's servants had slain him. Amalickiah, through fraud and deceit, gained control of the entire Lamanite kingdom when he took the queen to wife.

12. MORIANTON'S[2] MAID SERVANT

Alma 50:30. **Morianton**[2] (#103), a man of much passion, angrily beat one of his **MAID SERVANTS**. This maid servant fled to the camp of **Moroni**[1] (#97). She told him about Morianton's[2] intentions to flee with his people to the land northward because they had been engaged in a property dispute with the people of Lehi. This knowledge allowed Moroni[1] to send **Teancum** (#104) and an army to head them off. A battle ensued in which Morianton[2] was killed.

13. LAMANITE GUARDS AT THE CITY OF GID

Alma 55:8. **Laman**[4] (#111), a Nephite soldier and descendant of **Laman**[1] (#3), was sought out by Moroni[1] (#97) to help free the Nephite prisoners who were surrounded by **LAMANITE GUARDS**. Laman[4] and a few men with him approached the guards. Laman[4] told him he was a Lamanite who had escaped from the Nephites and that they had taken of their wine and had it with them. Laman[4] suggested saving it until they go to battle against the Nephites. This just made the guards want it even more. This was Laman's[4] plan because the wine had been carefully prepared and was especially strong. The guards got drunk and fell asleep. Moroni[1] and his soldiers quietly tossed weapons in to the prisoners so they were all armed. The Nephite army then surrounded the Lamanite armies. Thus, in the morning, the Nephites were liberated without bloodshed. The Lamanites were taken prisoner and were made to strengthen the fortifications round about the city of Gid which the Nephites now controlled. The prisoners were then taken to Bountiful. From time to time the Lamanites attempted to encircle them about by night, but they only suffered losses themselves. Many times they attempted to trick the Nephites into drinking poisoned wine, but the Nephites couldn't be tricked.

14. AMMORON'S SERVANTS

Alma 62:36. **Teancum (#104),** a loyal Nephi military leader, killed **Ammoron** (#108), the brother of **Amalickiah** (#99), because he blamed these two for the great and lasting war between the Nephites and the Lamanites. However, when he cast a javelin through Ammoron's heart, Ammoron awakened his **SERVANTS** before he died, and they pursued Teancum and slew him.

15. HELAMAN'S SERVANT

Helaman 2:6. When **Helaman**[2] (#91) was appointed to fill the judgment-seat, **Kishkumen** (#122) sought to kill him. As he was on the way to accomplish his desire, one of **HELAMAN'S SERVANTS**, pretending to be part of this secret band, gave Kishkumen a sign. Kishkumen told the servant about his murderous plans and asked for help in getting to the judgment-seat. After the servant discovered Kishkumen's plans, he agreed to help him find the way to the judgment-seat. On the way, the servant stabbed Kishkumen in the heart.

16. FIVE MEN SENT TO VERIFY THE DEATH OF THE CHIEF JUDGE SEEZORAM

Helaman 9:1. When corrupt judges sought to incite the people against Nephi[2] (#127), he announced the murder of their chief judge **Seezoram** (#133). **FIVE OF THE MEN** in that gathering went to see if what Nephi[2] said was true. When these five men found the slain chief judge, they fell to the earth in amazement. When others came and saw the slain Seezoram and the five fallen men, they put the men in prison, blaming them for the murder. The next day, when the people assembled themselves together to fast and mourn, the judges who had been at the garden of Nephi[2] asked what had become of their five messengers. The judges had the five men who had been blamed for the murder brought before them and recognized that they were the five whom they had sent. Thus, they were set free.

17. AKISH'S OTHER SONS

Ether 9: 10. After **Akish** (#199) had gained the kingdom through murder and deceit, and after his son **Nimrah** (#202) had fled out of the land to dwell with **Omer** (#194), Akish had **OTHER SONS**. Even though they pledged to support him in his evil reign, they wanted power themselves. Therefore, they bought the people with money and in that way drew the great part of them away. They waged war upon their father. In the space of many years, all but thirty people were killed.

18. ROBBER

Ether 10:3. **Shez**[1] (#207) was a righteous Jaredite king. His son **Shez**[2] (#208) rose up against him and caused him much grief. However, Shez[2] was smitten by a **ROBBER** because of his riches, and peace was restored to Shez[1].

19. TWO PEOPLE REFERRED TO AS MIGHTY MEN

Ether 11:15-16. **A MIGHTY MAN** in iniquity, a participant in secret combinations, rose up and gave battle unto **Moron** (#229). He overthrew half the kingdom and ruled that half for many years. Eventually Moron overthrew him and regained that half of the kingdom. However, **ANOTHER MIGHTY MAN** rose up, a descendant of the brother of **Jared**[2] (#181), and he overthrew Moron and obtained the kingdom. Moron dwelt in captivity all the rest of his days.

20. GILEAD'S HIGH PRIEST

Ether 14:9. **Gilead** (#236) was killed by his <u>**HIGH PRIEST**</u> as he sat upon the throne. This high priest was killed shortly thereafter by **Lib**[2] (#237), a member of the secret combinations.

Supplement A

BIBLICAL PEOPLE REFERRED TO IN THE BOOK OF MORMON

In Order of Their Appearance

SA #1. ZEDEKIAH[1]

1 Nephi 1:4. <u>**ZEDEKIAH**</u>[1] was the last king of Judah [c. 600 B.C.]. [**Zedekiah**[2] was one of the twelve Nephite disciples.] It was in the first year of the reign of Zedekiah[1] that **Lehi**[1] (#1) was warned by the Lord to leave Jerusalem because of the wickedness of the people. The brass plates contain the record of the Jews to the beginning of Zedekiah's[1] reign. **Mulek** (#49), Zedekiah's[1] son, was the only one of Zedekiah's[1] sons that was not slain. **Zarahemla** (#29) was a descendant of Mulek. The people of Zarahemla came from Jerusalem at the time Zedekiah[1] was taken captive to Babylon.

SA #2. MOSES

1 Nephi 4:2. <u>**MOSES**</u> was a great Hebrew prophet who lived about the 15th century B.C. His history is recorded in the Old Testament.

SA #3. PHARAOH

1 Nephi 4:2. <u>**PHARAOH**</u> was the title for the rulers of ancient Egypt. One sent his armies after **Moses** (SA #2) when Moses led the children of Israel out of bondage. The Pharaoh's armies were drowned in the Red Sea.

SA #4. ADAM

1 Nephi 5:11. <u>ADAM</u> was the first man created on earth; the father of all mankind. He and his wife **Eve** (SA #5) were driven from the Garden of Eden after they partook of the forbidden fruit.

SA #5. EVE

1 Nephi 5:11. <u>EVE</u> was the first woman created on earth; the mother of all mankind. She and her husband **Adam** (SA #4) were driven from the Garden of Eden after they partook of the forbidden fruit.

SA #6. JEREMIAH[1]

1 Nephi 5:13. <u>JEREMIAH</u>[1] was a Hebrew prophet who was cast into prison by the people. He was a contemporary of **Lehi**[1] (#1). [**Jeremiah**[2] (#150) was one of the twelve Nephite disciples.]

SA #7. JOSEPH[1]

1 Nephi 5:14. <u>JOSEPH</u>[1] was the son of **Jacob**[1] (SA #8) and was carried into Egypt. **Lehi**[1] (#1) was a descendant of Joseph[1] and father of **Joseph**[2] (#11). **Laban** (#7) and **Aminadi** (#67) were descendants of Joseph[1].

2 Nephi 3:7-15. Joseph[1] testified of a latter-day seer named **Joseph** [Supplement C].

SA #8. JACOB[1]

1 Nephi 5:14. <u>JACOB</u>[1] was the father of the twelve tribes. His name was changed by the Lord to Israel. [**Jacob**[2] (#10) was the son of **Lehi**[1] (#1). **Jacob**[3] (#109) was an apostate Nephite. **Jacob**[4] (#142) was also an apostate Nephite.]

SA #9. ISAAC

1 Nephi 6:4. ISAAC was the son of **Abraham** (SA #16). Abraham was commanded to sacrifice Isaac unto the Lord, but the Lord provided a substitute sacrifice. Abraham's offering of Isaac is a similitude of God and his Son.

SA #10. JOHN THE BELOVED

1 Nephi 14:20. JOHN THE BELOVED is also known as **JOHN THE REVELATOR. Nephi**[1] (#6) beheld John in vision.

3 Nephi 28. **Three of the Nephite disciples** desired to tarry on the earth, as did John the beloved.

Ether 4. The time will come when the revelations which have been written by John will be unfolded in the eyes of all the people [v. 16].

SA #11. ISAIAH[1]

1 Nephi 15:20. ISAIAH[1] was a Hebrew prophet [c. 740 B.C.] and was the **son of Amoz** (SA #18). He is quoted extensively in The Book of Mormon. [**Isaiah**[2] (#154) was one of the twelve Nephite disciples.]

SA #12. ZENOCK

1 Nephi 19:10. ZENOCK was a prophet of Israel known to the **Nephites** (#13). He had prophesied of the crucifixion of the **Savior** (#143).

Alma 33:17. He was rejected by the people and stoned to death.

SA #13. NEUM

1 Nephi 19:10. NEUM was a Hebrew prophet quoted by **Nephi**[1] (#6). He, too, had prophesied of the crucifixion of the **Savior** (#143).

SA #14. ZENOS

1 Nephi 19:10. **ZENOS** was a prophet of Israel known to the **Nephites** (#13). **Nephi**[1] (#6) quoted him regarding the three days of darkness which would be given as a sign at the time of the **Savior's** (#143) crucifixion.

Jacob 5. **Jacob**[2] (#10) quoted Zenos' parable of the tame and wild olive trees.

Helaman 8:19. Zenos was slain for testifying boldly of Christ.

SA #15. SOLOMON

2 Nephi 5:16. **SOLOMON** was a king of Israel, the son of **David** (SA #21). He built a magnificent temple. He had many wives and concubines, which was abominable before the Lord.

SA #16. ABRAHAM

2 Nephi 8:2. **ABRAHAM** was the father of **Isaac** (SA #9). He is the father of the faithful. The Lord redeemed Abraham.

Jacob 4. He was obedient when commanded to sacrifice Isaac [v. 5].

Alma 5. Murderers cannot sit in the kingdom with Abraham [v. 24].

Alma 13. Abraham paid tithes to **Melchizedek** (SA #27) [v. 15].

Helaman 8. Abraham and other Old Testament prophets testified of the **Son** (#143) [vs. 16-17].

SA #17. SARAH, SARAI

2 Nephi 8:2. **SARAH** (also called **SARAI**) was the wife of **Abraham** (SA #16).

SA #18. AMOZ

2 Nephi 12:1. <u>AMOZ</u> was the father of **Isaiah**[1] (SA #11) [c. 800 B.C.]

SA #19. MAHER-SHALAL-HASH-BAZ

2 Nephi 18:1. <u>MAHER-SHALAL-HASH-BAZ</u> was the son of **Isaiah**[1] (SA #11). His mother was a prophetess [v. 3]. Isaiah[1] was commanded to write concerning his son.

SA #20. PROPHETESS

2 Nephi 18:3. The **PROPHETESS** bore **Maher-shalal-hash-baz** (SA #19), the son of **Isaiah**[1] (SA #11).

SA #21. DAVID

2 Nephi 19:7. <u>DAVID</u> was a king of Israel and the father of **Solomon** (SA #15). **Isaiah**[1] (SA #11) said there would be no end to the throne of David. His practice of having many wives and concubines was abominable before the Lord.

SA #22. MANASSEH

2 Nephi 19:21. <u>MANASSEH</u> was the elder son of **Joseph**[1] (SA #7). His brother was **Ephraim** (SA #23). At the blessing by Jacob[1], Ephraim, though the second son, was set before Manasseh. [See the *Bible Dictionary*.]

Alma 10. **Lehi**[1] was a descendant of Manasseh [v. 3].

SA #23. EPHRAIM

2 Nephi 19:21. <u>EPHRAIM</u> was the second son of **Joseph**[1] (SA #7). His elder brother was **Manasseh** (SA #22). At the blessing by Jacob[1], Ephraim was set before Manasseh. [See the *Bible Dictionary*.]

SA #24. JESSE

2 Nephi 21:1. <u>**JESSE**</u> was the father of **David** (SA #21) and ancestor of all the kings of Judah and also of **Christ** (#143). [See the *Bible Dictionary.*]

SA #25. MARY

1 Nephi 11:13. <u>**MARY**</u> is not referred to by name in this scripture, but is the virgin **Nephi**[1] (#6) referred to when he said he saw in a vision "a virgin," and she was exceedingly fair and white.
Mosiah 3:8. Mary was the mother of **Jesus** (#143), the Son of God.

Alma 7:10. **Alma**[2] (#50) prophesied that the Son of God would be born of Mary, at Jerusalem. She would be a virgin and would conceive by the power of the Holy Ghost.

SA #26. NOAH[1]

Alma 10:22. <u>**NOAH**</u>[1] was the patriarch at the time of the flood. After leading Noah[1] and his family to safety via the ark, the Lord promised Noah[1] that he would not destroy the earth by flood again. [**Noah**[2] (#190) was a wicked Jaredite; **Noah**[3] (#40) a wicked Nephite.]

Ether 6. The Jaredite vessels were tight, like the ark of Noah[1].

SA #27. MELCHIZEDEK

Alma 13:14. <u>**MELCHIZEDEK**</u> was a high priest after the order of God, and **Abraham** (SA #16) paid his tithes to him. He was also the king of Salem. He was called the prince of peace because he brought his people who were very wicked to a state of righteousness when he preached repentance to them. He reigned under his father. There were many priests both before and after him, but none greater than he; thus, special mention is made of him in the scriptures.

SA #28. CAIN

Helaman 6:27. <u>CAIN</u> was the son of **Adam** (SA #4) and **Eve** (SA #5). He plotted with Lucifer to kill his brother **Abel** (SA #29).

Ether 8. He was a murderer, and he handed down the secret oaths.

SA #29. ABEL

Helaman 6:27. <u>ABEL</u> was the son of **Adam** (SA #4) and **Eve** (SA #5). **Cain** (SA #28), his brother, plotted with Satan to kill him.

SA #30. SAMUEL[1]

3 Nephi 20:24. <u>SAMUEL</u>[1] was a Hebrew prophet. He and all prophets have testified of **Christ** (#143). [**Samuel**[2] (#135) was a prophet known as **Samuel the Lamanite**.]

SA #31. MALACHI

3 Nephi 24:1. <u>MALACHI</u> was a Jewish prophet around the late fifth century B.C. The resurrected **Savior** (#143) quoted some of his prophecies to the people in the land of Bountiful.

SA #32. LEVI[1]

3 Nephi 24:3. <u>LEVI</u>[1] was one of **Jacob's**[1] (SA #8) twelve sons. [**Levi**[2] (#213) was a righteous Jaredite.]

SA #33. ELIJAH

3 Nephi 25:5. **ELIJAH** was a prophet of Israel about 900 B.C. The Lord said, "Behold, I will send you Elijah the prophet before the great and dreadful day of the Lord."

SA #34. NIMROD[1]

Ether 2:1. **NIMROD**[1] was the grandson of Ham (Old Testatment), who was the son of **Noah**[1] (SA #26). He was a mighty hunter. The Jaredites temporarily dwelt in a valley named after Nimrod[1]. [**Nimrod**[2] (#193) was a righteous Jaredite.]

Supplement B

ALPHABETICAL LISTING OF BIBLICAL PEOPLE NOT MENTIONED IN THE BOOK OF MORMON

But Who Share Names with Book of Mormon People

SB #1. Aaron[1] **AARON**[1] was the brother of Moses.

SB #2. Enos[1] **ENOS**[1] was a grandson of Adam and Eve.

SB #3. Jared[1] **JARED**[1] was the father of Enoch[2].

SB #4. Nehor[1] **NEHOR**[1] was the brother of Abraham.

SB #5. Seth[1] **SETH**[1] was the son of Adam and Eve.

SB #6. Shem[1] **SHEM**[1] was the son of Noah[1].

Supplement C

JOSEPH SMITH, JR., TRANSLATOR OF
THE BOOK OF MORMON

Joseph[1] (SA #7), son of **Jacob**[1] (SA #8) and sold by his brothers and carried into Egypt as a slave, prophesied of **Joseph Smith, Jr.,** a latter-day seer. [2 Nephi 3:6-19.]

"For Joseph truly testified, saying: A seer [Joseph Smith, Jr.] shall the Lord my God raise up, who shall be a choice seer unto the fruit of my loins.

"Yea, Joseph truly said: Thus saith the Lord unto me: A choice seer will I raise up out of the fruit of thy loins; and he shall be esteemed highly among the fruit of thy loins. And unto him will I give commandment that he shall do a work for the fruit of thy loins, his brethren, which shall be of great worth unto them, even to the bringing of them to the knowledge of the covenants which I have made with thy fathers.

"And I will give unto him a commandment that he shall do none other work, save the work which I shall command him. And I will make him great in mine eyes; for he shall do my work.

"And he shall be great like unto Moses, whom I have said I would raise up unto you, to deliver my people, O house of Israel.

"And Moses will I raise up, to deliver thy people out of the land of Egypt.

"But a seer [Joseph Smith, Jr.] will I raise up out of the fruit of thy loins; and unto him will I give power to bring forth my word [The Book of Mormon] unto the seed of thy loins—and not to the bringing forth my word only, saith the Lord, but to the convincing them of my word, which shall have already gone forth among them.

"Wherefore, the fruit of thy loins shall write; and the fruit of the loins of Judah shall write; and that which shall be written by the fruit of thy loins [The Book of Mormon], and also that which shall be written by the fruit of the loins of Judah [the Bible], shall grow together, unto the confounding of false doctrines and laying down of contentions, and establishing peace among the fruit of thy loins, and bringing them to the knowledge of their fathers in the latter days, and also to the knowledge of my covenants, saith the Lord.

"And out of weakness he shall be made strong, in that day when my work shall commence among all my people, unto the restoring thee, O house of Israel, saith the Lord.

"And thus prophesied Joseph, saying; Behold, that seer will the Lord bless; and they that seek to destroy him shall be confounded; for this promise, which I have obtained of the Lord, of the fruit of my loins, shall be fulfilled. Behold, I am sure of the fulfilling of this promise;

"And his name [Joseph Smith, Jr.] shall be called after me [Joseph]; and it shall be after the name of his father [Joseph Smith, Sr.]. And he shall be like unto me; for the thing, which the Lord shall bring forth by his hand, by the power of the Lord shall bring my people unto salvation.

"Yea, thus prophesied Joseph: I am sure of this thing, even as I am sure of the promise of Moses; for the Lord hath said unto me, I will preserve thy seed forever.

"And the Lord hath said: I will raise up a Moses; and I will give power unto him in a rod; and I will give judgment unto him in writing. Yet I will not loose his tongue, that he shall speak much, for I will not make him mighty in speaking. But I will write unto him my law, by the finger of mine own hand; and I will make a spokesman for him.

"And the Lord said unto me also: I will raise up unto the fruit of thy loins; and I will make for him a spokesman. And I, behold, I will give unto him that he shall write the writing of the fruit of thy loins, unto the fruit of thy loins; and the spokesman of thy loins shall declare it.

"And the words which he shall write shall be the words which are expedient in my wisdom should go forth unto the fruit of thy loins. And it shall be as if the fruit of thy loins had cried unto them from the dust; for I know their faith."

Time Line of Record Keepers

Note: The record keepers are highlighted with bold lettering.

600 b.c.   **Lehi[1] and family leave Jerusalem.**
                  Nephi[1] makes a record. [1 Nephi 1:2]
600 - 592 B.C.   Lehi[1] and his group travel in the wilderness. **They**
                  carry the brass plates of Laban with them.
                  Joseph[2] and Jacob[2] are born in the wilderness.
                  Ishmael[1] dies. [1 Nephi 16:34]
About 591 B.C.   The Lord instructs Nephi[1] to build a ship.
About 592 B.C.   They reach the promised land.
Between 588-
570 B.C.   Lehi[1] dies. [2 Nephi 4:12]
                  Nephi[1] and his followers separate themselves from
                  the Lamanites. [2 Nephi 5:6]
About 570 -
569 B.C.   Nephi[1] consecrates Joseph[2] and Jacob[2] to be priests
                       and teachers. [2 Nephi 5:26]
544 b.c.   **Nephi[1] gives the records to Jacob[2].** [Jacob 1:1]
                  Nephi[1] dies. [Jacob 1:12]
544-421 b.c.   **Jacob[2] turns the records over to Enos[2].** [Jacob 7:27]
                  Jacob[2] dies.
About 420 b.c.   **Enos[2] turns the records over to Jarom.** [Enos 1:25]
                  Enos[2] dies.
361 b.c.   **Jarom gives the records to Omni.** [Jarom 1:15]
317 b.c.   **Omni gives the records to Amaron.** [Omni 1:3]
279 b.c.   **Amaron gives the records to Chemish.** [Omni 1:8]
279 - 130 b.c.   **Chemish gives the records to Abinadom.** [Omni 1:10]
                  Abinadom gives the records to Amaleki[1]. [Omni 1:12]
                  Amaleki[1] lives to see Mosiah's[1] death.
                  Mosiah's[1] son Benjamin reigns in his stead.
                  Amaleki[1] gives records to king Benjamin. [Omni 1:25]
200 B.C.   Zeniff and a group go up into the wilderness.
160 B.C.   Zeniff confers the kingdom on his son Noah[3].
                  [Mosiah 10:22]

About 150 B.C.	Abinadi preaches to Noah[3] and his people.
	Alma[1] believes Abinadi.
About 147 B.C.	Alma[1] baptizes in the Waters of Mormon.
145 - 121 B.C.	Alma[1] refuses to be king. [Mosiah 23:7]
	Amulon, leader of the priests of Noah[1], persecutes Alma[1] and his people. [Mosiah 24:9]
145 - 122 B.C.	King Noah[3] is burned to death, fulfilling Abinadi s prophecy. [Mosiah 19:20]
About 124 b.c.	**King Benjamin passes the records on to Mosiah[2].** Mosiah[2] is 30 years old. [Mosiah 1:16]
About 121 B.C.	King Benjamin dies.
	Mosiah[2] sends 16 men up to the land of Lehi-Nephi. Ammon[1], a descendant of Zarahemla, goes with them. Amaleki[1], Helem and Hem go with him. They discover king Limhi [Zeniff's grandson] and his people. Limhi reigns over the more righteous part of the people. Ammon[1] and king Limhi plan for escape from Lamanite bondage. Gideon proposes a plan. [Mosiah 22:6]
About 120 B.C.	The Lord leads Alma[1] and his people back to Zarahemla where they join king Mosiah[2]. [Mosiah 24:25]
Probably 120 - 100 B.C.	Alma[1] has authority over the church.
Probably 100 - 92 B.C.	Alma[2] and Mosiah's[2] sons persecute the church. They are visited by an angel, and henceforth become missionaries. [Mosiah 27:8-32]
About 92 b.c.	The sons of Mosiah[2] begin their 14 year missionary expedition to preach to the Lamanites. [Mosiah 28:9] Mosiah[2] translates the records on the plates of brass and causes to be written the records which were on the plates of gold which Limhi's people had found. [Mosiah 28:11] **Mosiah[2] confers records upon Alma[2].** [Mosiah 28:20] The reign of the judges begins—the era of kings ends. [Mosiah 29:25, 39] Alma[2] is chosen to be the first judge. [Alma 29:42]
About 91 B.C.	Gideon is slain by Nehor[2]. [Alma 1:9]
About 87 B.C.	Amlici seeks to become king. [Alma 2:1]
83 B.C.	Alma[2] gives up the judgment-seat to Nephihah to devote more time to preaching—retains office of high priest. [Alma 4:17] Goes to preach in Zarahemla. [Alma 5:1]

About 82 B.C.	Amulek meets and joins Alma². [Alma 8:20]
77 B.C.	The sons of Mosiah² meet up with Alma² on the way back to Zarahemla after their 14 years of missionary work with the Lamanites. [Alma 27:16] The converted Lamanites, the Anti-Nephi-Lehies, are with them.
74 B.C.	17th year of the judges. Korihor contends with Alma². Zerahemnah, leader of the Lamanites, comes against Alma² and his people. [Alma 43:5]
armies	Moroni¹ is appointed chief captain of the Nephite at age 25. [Alma 43:16]
About 73 B.C.	Alma² gives blessings and counsel to his sons. [Alma 36-42]
	Alma² has Helaman² take charge of the records. [Alma 37:1]
	Helaman² preaches to the people.
72 B.C.	Amalickiah causes problems. [Alma 46:3; 47] He has Lehonti murdered and the Lamanite king stabbed to death. He marries the queen and becomes leader of the Lamanites.
68 B.C.	24th year of the judges. Morianton causes problems.
67 B.C.	Rise of the king-men. [Alma 51:5]
About 60 B.C.	Moroni¹ yields up command of armies to his son Moronihah¹. [Alma 62:43]
	Pahoran¹ returns to the judgment-seat [Alma 62:44]
	Helaman² returns to preaching.
57 B.C.	35th year of the judges. Helaman² dies. [Alma 62:52]
56 b.c.	**Shiblon takes possession of the records.** [Alma 63:1]
55 B.C.	A northward migration begins. Hagoth builds ships.
53 b.c.	Shiblon dies. [Alma 63:10]
	Shiblon gives the records to Helaman³ before he dies. [Alma 63:11]
52 B.C.	Rise of Kishkumen and the Gadianton robbers. [Helaman 1:9]
50 B.C.	Helaman³ is appointed to fill the judgment-seat. [Helaman 2:2]

39 B.C.	Helaman[3] dies and his son Nephi[2] reigns in his stead. [Helaman 3:37]
6 B.C.	Samuel[2] the Lamanite prophesies of the coming of Christ. He describes signs signaling Christ's birth and also signs to occur at Christ's death. [Helaman 13-14]
A.D. 1	91 years have passed since the beginning of the judges. 600 years have passed since Lehi[1] left Jerusalem. Nephi[2] has departed. [3 Nephi 1:1-2]
	Nephi[3] has been given charge of the records. Commencement of 92nd year. Prophecies begin to be fulfilled. A day has been designated when believers will be put to death if the prophecies are not fulfilled by then. The Lord speaks to Nephi[3]—he will come into the world on the morrow. [3 Nephi 1:4-13]
A.D. 30	Wickedness destroys the government. The last chief judge is murdered. The people return to tribes. [3 Nephi 7:1-2]
A.D. 34	Signs signaling Christ's death begin to be fulfilled: earthquakes, fires, three days of darkness. [3 Nephi 8:5] The voice of the Savior is heard. [3 Nephi 9:1] The Savior appears to the Nephites in Bountiful after his death and resurrection; he ministers to the people. [3 Nephi 11:8]
A.D. 111	**Nephi[4] passes the records to his son Amos[1].** **Amos[1] keeps the records for 84 years.** [4 Nephi 1:19]
A.D. 195	Amos[1] dies. [4 Nephi 1:21] **Amos[2] keeps the records.**
A.D. 231	A division occurs among the people.
A.D. 306	Amos[2] dies. **Ammaron keeps the record.** [4 Nephi 1:47]
A.D. 321	Ammaron hides up the record.
About A.D. 322	**Ammaron instructs Mormon[2] to dig up the record when he's older and to record all that he observes.** [Mormon 1:2-4]

a.d. 345   **Mormon² gets the records.** [Mormon 2:17]

About A.D. 385   Mormon² is killed in the final battle at Cumorah.

                    Moroni² keeps the last record. [Mormon 8:1]

About A.D. 421   **Moroni² finishes the record and hides it up.**

A.D. 1827   **Joseph Smith, Jr. receives the record from the angel Moroni.** Note: After completing the translation of The Book of Mormon, Joseph Smith, Jr. returned the plates to the angel Moroni as he was instructed to do.

Index

ALPHABETICAL LISTING OF PEOPLE MENTIONED IN THE BOOK OF MORMON

Book of Mormon People	*Biblical People Mentioned in The Book of Mormon*	*Biblical People Not Mentioned in The Book of Mormon, But Whose Names Are The Same As Some Book of Mormon People*
A		
219. Aaron², p. 172	SA #29. Abel, p. 192	SB #1. Aaron¹, p. 194
52. Aaron³, p. 73	SA #16. Abraham, p. 190	
161. Aaron⁴, p. 151	SA # 4. Adam, p. 187	
44. Abinadi, p. 56	SA #18. Amoz, p. 190	
25. Abinadom, p. 42		
76. Abish, p. 88		
73. Aha, p. 86		
227. Ahah, p. 173		
199. Akish, p. 167		
201. Akish's Son, p. 167		
45. Alma¹, p. 58		
50. Alma², p. 62		
26. Amaleki¹, p. 42		
36. Amaleki², p. 50		
81. Amalekites, p. 90		
99. Amalickiah, p. 109		
101. Amalickiahites, p. 110		
23. Amaron, p. 42		
223. Amgid, p. 172		
130. Aminadab, p. 130		
67. Aminadi, p. 83		
56. Amlici, p. 78		
57. Amlicites, p. 79		
78. Ammah, p. 89		

L

M

O

P

Q

R

S

T

U-V-W-X-Y

Z

Notes:

a: Jeneum (#167) is spelled Jeneam in the Index to The Book of Mormon. However, in Mormon 6:14, it is spelled Jeneum.

b: In the Index to The Book of Mormon, there are two Ishmaels: Ishmael¹ (#9) and Ishmael² (#66). However, there is also an Ishmael in the Bible who is not mentioned in The Book of Mormon, nor is he listed in the Index. The Biblical Ishmael was Abraham's first son, by Hagar, Sarah's handmaiden. Technically, he should have the superscript number 1. Ishmael¹ (#9) should bear the superscript number 2; Ishmael² (#66) should bear the superscript number 3.

c: In the Index to The Book of Mormon, Heth¹ (#206) and Heth² (#218) are mislabeled. Heth¹, the early Jaredite, was the son of Com¹. Heth², the middle Jaredite, was the son of Hearthom.